Explaining Evil

ALSO AVAILABLE FROM BLOOMSBURY

God, Existence, and Fictional Objects, by John-Mark L. Miravalle
Wittgenstein, Religion and Ethics, edited by Mikel Burley
Philosophy of the Bhagavad Gita, by Keya Maitra
The Selected Writings of Maurice O'Connor Drury,
edited by John Hayes

Explaining Evil

Four Views

Edited by W. Paul Franks

BLOOMSBURY ACADEMIC
LONDON • NEW YORK • OXFORD • NEW DELHI • SYDNEY

BLOOMSBURY ACADEMIC
Bloomsbury Publishing Plc
50 Bedford Square, London, WC1B 3DP, UK
1385 Broadway, New York, NY 10018, USA

BLOOMSBURY, BLOOMSBURY ACADEMIC and the Diana logo are trademarks
of Bloomsbury Publishing Plc

First published in Great Britain 2019

Cover design by Eleanor Rose
Cover image © Getty Images

A catalogue record for this book is available from the British Library.

A catalog record for this book is available from the Library of Congress.

ISBN: HB: 978-1-5013-3114-5
PB: 978-1-5013-3112-1
ePDF: 978-1-5013-3115-2
eBook: 978-1-5013-3113-8

Typeset by Deanta Global Publishing Services, Chennai, India
Printed and bound in Great Britain

To find out more about our authors and books visit www.bloomsbury.com
and sign up for our newsletters.

In memory of W.H.F.

CONTENTS

NOTES ON CONTRIBUTORS

Richard Brian Davis is Professor of Philosophy at Tyndale University College. Professor Davis has published over thirty journal articles/book chapters and five books. Some of the latter include *Four Views on Christianity and Philosophy* (Zondervan, 2016), *Loving God with Your Mind: Essays in Honor of J.P. Moreland* (Moody, 2014), *24 and Philosophy* (Blackwell, 2007), and *The Metaphysics of Theism and Modality* (Peter Lang, 2001).

Paul Helm is the former professor of the History and Philosophy of Religion at King's College, London. He has authored numerous journal articles and books including: *Calvin: A Guide for the Perplexed* (T&T Clark, 2008), *Faith with Reason* (Cambridge, 2000), *Belief Policies* (Cambridge, 1994), *The Providence of God* (IVP Academic, 1994), and *Eternal God: A Study of God without Time* (Oxford, 1988).

Michael Ruse is Professor of Philosophy at Florida State University. Professor Ruse has published numerous journal articles/book chapters and authored or edited over fifty books. Some of his more recent books include: *Darwinism as Religion: What Literature Tells Us about Evolution* (Oxford, 2017), *The Cambridge Handbook to Evolutionary Ethics* (2017), *Science and Religion in Conflict?* (Oxford, 2016), *Atheism: What Everyone Needs to Know* (Oxford, 2015), and *The Cambridge Encyclopedia of Darwin and Evolutionary Thought* (Cambridge, 2013).

Erik J. Wielenberg is Professor of Philosophy at DePauw University. He has authored three books: *Robust Ethics: The Metaphysics and Epistemology of Godless Normative Realism* (Oxford, 2014), *God and the Reach of Reason: C.S. Lewis, David Hume, and Bertrand Russell* (Cambridge, 2008), and *Value and Virtue in a Godless Universe* (Cambridge, 2005), and over thirty journal articles/book chapters.

ACKNOWLEDGMENTS

Many people are deserving of thanks for this book becoming a reality. I am deeply grateful for the hard work of each of the authors who not only provided helpful insight into this topic, but also did so while not missing any of the deadlines a book of this nature demands. I have learned much about evil, and a host of associated issues, because of their thoughtful contributions. I would like to also thank two of my former professors: Linda Zagzebski, who was instrumental in helping me to think more clearly about the problem of evil, and Neera Badhwar, who first introduced me to the various issues concerning evil in general. Thanks are also due to the Faculty Research Committee at Tyndale University College for granting me a sabbatical during which I was, among other things, able to see this project to completion. Finally, I would like to thank my wife Tina Marie for her faithful support and encouragement, and my sons Alexander, Oliver, and Samuel who are a constant source of joy.

Introduction

W. Paul Franks

It is not terribly difficult to establish that the world contains evil. Unfortunately, it's all too easy to find yet another instance of immense harm befalling someone for no justifiable reason. While working on this introduction, the shooting at Marjory Stoneman Douglas High School in Parkland, FL, unfolded. Seventeen people, both students and teachers, were needlessly killed. Why do such terrible things occur? What about the various evils that result in far greater suffering, or even those that result in far less? When confronted with such evils it is commonplace, and natural, to seek out an explanation. Some explanations are meant to account for why some particular evil occurred, whereas others take a broader approach and are meant to give reasons for evil's existence in general. This book is focused on the latter task.

Establishing that there is evil is easy; determining *why* there is evil is a much more difficult task. Those familiar with the literature on the problem of evil will know that this has been a focus of Christian theists for centuries and with good reason. According to Christian theism, there is a being who exists apart from this universe, who cares about human welfare, and has a say in the goings-on of this universe. In addition, this being is said to be perfectly morally good, omniscient, and omnipotent. This alone is sufficient to give a rough approximation of what has come to be known as the problem of evil. Presumably, an omnipotent being would be able to prevent evil, an omniscient being would know how to prevent evil, and a perfectly good being would want to prevent evil. So why, then, is there evil?

In most contemporary discussions, problems like the one outlined above tend to amount to an argument for atheism since, it is alleged, one is incapable of justifying the belief that God exists given the evil we find in the world. It is in this context that we see the familiar distinction between *logical* and *evidential* problems of evil. As Daniel Howard-Snyder has pointed out, these labels can be somewhat misleading since evidential problems tend to make rigorous use of logical structure, especially in terms of probabilities, and logical problems are often used as evidence that counts against theism (1996, xii). Still, with this qualification in mind, the distinction is useful. Briefly put, the evidential problem attempts to demonstrate that, given the existence of evil, it is more likely that there is not a God than that there is a God, whereas the logical problem attempts to demonstrate that the existence of evil is logically incompatible with the very notion of God.[1] Advocates of either type of problem claim that the argument gives an individual reason to believe that God does not exist.

As one would expect, Christian theists have not remained silent on this issue and there is no shortage of responses to these problems.[2] However, before going any further it is important to note that this is not a book dealing with solutions to the problem of evil in either its logical or evidential forms. In fact, other than the brief synopsis above, you won't find the problem of evil defended, refuted, or even stated. While the four authors contributing to this book are grappling with the presence of evil in this world, they are not doing so only in the context of evil somehow generating a problem for theism. There are two reasons for this. First, the task of explaining evil is not something that falls to theists alone. Upon learning of another mass shooting or terrorist attack, theists aren't the only ones wondering why such things occur. Non-theists are just as prone to seek out explanations for evil as anyone else.

The second reason for taking a different approach than many "problem of evil" books follows closely on the first. In many discussions about the problem of evil it's not uncommon for the participants to never get around to stating what they believe are the actual reasons for evil. Instead, what often happens is that an atheist lays out what appears to be a problem for theism, and theists too easily content themselves with focusing on some alleged problem with that problem for theism. While this is a worthwhile activity, taken alone it doesn't actually give us what we were initially looking for—an explanation for evil. Instead of simply focusing on problems with other accounts of evil, the aim of this book is for each contributor to present his own positive account of evil and then also be able to respond to criticisms to it.

While this is not a typical book on the problem of evil, it is certainly still relevant to that topic. Those seeking theistic solutions to the problem of evil will find in Paul Helm and Richard Brian Davis resources for that task, even though resolving an argument against theism is not their primary aim. So, in some sense, these two theistic contributors will add to the ever-growing literature on the problem of evil, but they go about doing so in a different way. Their primary goal is to show how evil fits within their theistic worldview. That is, for both Davis and Helm the question to answer is not "Given evil, how can there be a God?" but instead, "Given God, how can there be evil?"[3]

This way of thinking about evil also extends to the two atheistic contributors: Michael Ruse and Erik J. Wielenberg.[4] Of course, as atheists, they aren't concerned with explaining evil's existence given that God exists. But, there remains a need to explain evil's existence given their atheism. Typically, when non-theists write on the problem of evil they do so in an attempt to establish that there is no God, but what is often missing are *their* explanations for evil. One might be tempted to just say that evil happens because we live in a world that pays no special attention to us. That is, we are no different in any significant way from the rest of the universe so we too are subject to the whims of nature and to the evil acts of other human beings. While I'm sure many non-theists believe something along these lines, one may still wonder why we should think of all that as *evil*. Given atheism, how does one maintain that instances of pain and suffering are in fact evil? Why are human persons so adept at intentionally causing the suffering of both humans and animals? Does the concept "evil" require, as many theists maintain, some sort of objective moral order? If so, can non-theism support such a thing? If it's not required, then how should we think about evil? These are the kinds of concerns that Ruse and Wielenberg address.

A word on "Evil"

Before continuing any further, a word or two on the term "evil" is in order. We use the word in a wide variety of ways and so it can be difficult to state precisely what it is that makes something or someone evil. This, it seems, is why few philosophers of religion working on the problem of evil ever bother defining it.[5] Instead of defining it, we are often given various examples of evil and then those examples are classified into categories. Consider, for example, Alvin Plantinga's discussion of evil in *God and Other Minds*:

> A distinction must be made between *moral evil* and *physical evil*. The former, roughly, is the evil which results from human choice or volition; the latter is that which does not. Suffering due to an earthquake, for example, would be physical evil; suffering resulting from human cruelty would be moral evil. This distinction, of course, is not very clear and many questions could be raised about it; but perhaps it is not necessary to deal with these questions here. (1967, 132)

The distinction between moral and physical—or sometimes "natural"—evil is useful, but it doesn't actually say much about what evil is.[6] Instead, it tells us that whatever evil is, it can be caused by human agents or by some act of nature. This way of thinking about evil, especially when considering the problem of evil, is certainly not unique to Plantinga. It's not much of a stretch to say that this is far more common than not.

For example, nearly fifty years after *God and Other Minds* was published, we see Chad Meister taking the same basic approach. After first noting that "it is difficult, if not downright impossible, to provide a clear and concise definition [of evil]," he then moves on to classify evil in much the same way as Plantinga. He continues, "A standard classification of evil divides it into two broad types: moral and natural. Some examples may help to distinguish them" (2012, 2–3). Perhaps when it comes to the problem of evil a more precise account just isn't needed. Perhaps all we need to do to raise the problem of evil is point to various states of affairs that involve immense suffering and ask "Why does God allow *that?*" This may be so; however it is worth noting that philosophers who work on evil generally—that is, those who aren't primarily concerned with the problem of evil—don't seem as hesitant to attempt a definition.

In his book, *The Roots of Evil*, John Kekes is anything but hesitant to provide what he takes to be a complete account of what makes something evil. He writes,

> The evil of an action, therefore, consists in the combination of three components: the malevolent motivation of evildoers;

the serious, excessive harm caused by their actions; and the lack of a morally acceptable excuse for the actions. Each of these components is necessary, and they are jointly sufficient for condemning an action as evil. (2005, 2)

Here we have a clearly stated set of necessary and sufficient conditions for determining whether some action is evil. Kekes, however, is not alone. Todd Calder has claimed to pick out the "essential properties" of an evil action. Such properties include "a victim's significant harm" and a perpetrator's "inexcusable intention to bring about, allow, or witness, significant harm for an unworthy goal" (2013, 194). While both Kekes and Calder talk about evil in reference to harm caused, Daryl Koehn takes a different approach. According to Koehn, "Evil is frustrated desire stemming from our efforts to preserve a false conception of the self" (2005, 4). For Koehn, this provides a fuller account of evil because it serves to explain the cause of evil itself. The point here is not to adjudicate between these accounts of evil, but instead to note that philosophers working on the problem of evil may learn something interesting about evil by looking to those whose work is focused on evil in general.

For example, in light of the above discussion about moral and natural evils, one may wonder how these general accounts deal with natural evil. None of the three, it seems, have anything whatsoever to do with natural evil, as defined by Plantinga and Meister. In light of this one might simply state that the failure of these accounts in this regard means that they are not adequate conceptions of evil. However, one might also go in the other direction. Because harms caused by moral agents are just so different from harms caused by acts of nature, it may be better to dispense with the term "natural evil" altogether.[7] Evil just is a moral notion and so the suffering caused by natural events isn't evil at all. This is precisely what Calder has suggested elsewhere:

No matter how much harm a hurricane, a falling tree, or a volcano might cause humans or animals, such harm does not admit of moral explanation in the absence of agency, and thus is not evil. (2002, 51)[8]

It's not that such events do not cause pain and suffering, it's just that such pain and suffering isn't *evil*.

One advantage of distinguishing the problem of *evil* from the problem of *nature-based suffering* (for lack of a better phrase) is that it helps make evident that there are two different kinds of problems related to suffering. If nothing else, this is another way in which this is not simply a book on the problem of evil. As you will soon see, each of the four authors' explanations of evil focus primarily, if not exclusively, on the moral variety. Although theists may still need to explain why God would permit such suffering, keeping the two problems distinct also makes it easier to see that a solution to one may have nothing at all to do with a solution to the other.[9] Separating the two also makes it easier for non-theists, who may not think there is a problem of nature-based suffering at all, to nevertheless fully engage in the project of explaining evil. So, for example, when Ruse writes in his lead essay that natural evil is not a problem at all (85), that doesn't mean he is offering any less of an explanation for evil than the theist.

Let us now turn to a synopsis of each chapter.

Summary of the discussion

The four contributors have authored a truly impressive number of important books and articles in metaphysics, epistemology, ethics, philosophy of religion, and theology. Given the divergent views of the authors—atheism/theism, moral realism/non-realism, free will compatibilism/incompatibilism, divine determinism/indeterminism—it is my hope that the structure of the book will allow the reader to benefit from the significant interaction each contributor has with the others. Each chapter consists of a lead essay, three responses to the lead essay, and a final reply.

In Chapter 1, Richard Davis attempts to explain evil's presence by appeal to "agent-causal theism." Evil, properly understood, involves immoral thoughts, desires, decisions, and actions freely and purposefully entertained or undertaken to inflict or permit unjustifiable harms being committed. This presupposes that there are immaterial, conscious agents with the power to act as agent-causes: to originate volitions to act without being caused to do so. If that's right, Davis argues, we can see that certain worldviews will preclude the existence of evil, since they rule out consciousness and/or agent-causal freedom. Here he singles out for particular criticism

Darwinian Naturalism and Calvinistic Theism. Both are bereft of the resources, he says, to explain the existence of conscious rational agents with the power of self-motion. Neither, then, can account for the reality of evil. It is only if theism is true, we're told, that evil would even be a bare possibility. Strangely then, and contrary to one's initial expectations, the existence of evil implies that we live in a theistic universe.

In Chapter 2, Paul Helm's explanation for evil begins by disambiguating the question "Why evil?" This is necessary, he says, for in asking this question one might mean "What is God's purpose in permitting or ordaining evil?" or given that God is the ordainer "How does evil occur?" Helm's approach is one of "faith seeking understanding." Given the existence of God, we can say that the universe is arranged for the display of God's perfection. As such, we find in the universe moral evil because it makes necessary the incarnation. Borrowing from Alvin Plantinga's *felix culpa* theodicy, Helm argues that a world "including the incarnation of the Son of God is immeasurably better than one without it." In answering the second question Helm employs a compatibilistic account of freedom to show that human persons are responsible for having departed from their original condition (as created by God). Consequently, although they are determined by their nature and circumstances to think, decide, and act as they do, they are nevertheless responsible for causing all of the moral evil we see in the world.

Next we turn to two powerful non-theistic attempts to account for evil. According to Michael Ruse, while we have sufficient grounds for being moral skeptics, we can still maintain that there are evil actions perpetrated by evil people. Evil certainly has a value component to it, but this doesn't mean that we must turn to theism (contra Davis and Helm) nor to something akin to a Platonic form (contra Wielenberg) to explain it. Instead, Ruse looks to Charles Darwin's evolutionary account to explain evil's nature and origin. Human persons are capable of making choices, understood along compatibilist lines, and some of those choices bring about moral evil. This happens when a person goes against his or her "biologically given sense of morality." This morality is system-dependent, so that what is morally wrong for humans may not be morally wrong for other species. This shouldn't be surprising, however, since what is beneficial for the survival of one species may not be beneficial for others.

In the concluding chapter, Erik J. Wielenberg provides us with the second non-theistic account of evil. Wielenberg begins by spelling out how ethical properties, including evil, neither reduce to natural properties nor do they require the existence of a divine being. Instead, ethical properties are sui generis. They are "entirely different kinds of things from natural or supernatural properties." Having shown what evil is, Wielenberg moves on to uncover its cause. The property *being evil* is instantiated by nonethical properties, like *causing pain just for fun*, via a "robust causal relation" that holds between the two. To help determine *why* this occurs, Wielenberg turns to empirical research into dehumanization. This phenomenon is responsible for many instances of properties that directly robustly cause the nonnatural property *being evil*. There is no need for a natural or a supernatural explanation here. For states of affairs involving ethical properties like *being evil* are said to be basic ethical facts. Like mathematical truths, they are brute givens whose obtaining requires no external explanation.

Thus is the (probably too) brief overview of the lead chapters. If you are already familiar with the contributors, you likely won't be too surprised by their general approach. What I think you will find interesting is how they each apply their previous research into the particularly difficult issue of explaining evil. Each author, approaching the same question from a very different perspective, not only gives his account, but also has the opportunity to respond to each of the other lead essays. It is here that interesting "alliances" emerge. Though Helm and Ruse disagree on whether God exists, both find Davis's libertarian account of free will unsatisfactory. They both also explicitly affirm a type of compatibilism, but do so for very different reasons which, in turn, lead to their differences in explaining evil. While Ruse and Wielenberg both reject theism, and rely to varying extents on evolution to explain the occurrence of evil, when it comes to explaining the nature of morality, Wielenberg's objective account is more in line with the two theists than with Ruse.

Notes

1 See Howard-Snyder (1996) for a collection of evidential problems of evil. For a collection of classic problems of evil, including logical problems, see Adams and Adams (1991).

2 For a few of the more influential contemporary responses, see Plantinga (1974b), Swinburne (1998), Adams (1999), van Inwagen (2006), and Stump (2010).

3 This approach is similar to what Marilyn Adams and Robert Adams refer to as an *aporetic,* rather than an *atheological,* approach to the issue. See Adams and Adams (1991, 3–4). Murray and Greenberg (2016) note that the former was commonplace among Christian theists until the time of Leibniz, who was concerned with both.

4 Although Wielenberg refers to himself as an atheist, Ruse considers himself to be "atheistic about Christianity and agnostic about Ultimate Reality" (85). For the sake of simplicity, I will refer to them both as atheists.

5 One important exception to this is Langtry (2008, 42–47).

6 In the above quote we do see Plantinga *associate* evil with suffering, but it's not clear—nor does he claim—that "evil" just is "suffering." On the difference between the two, see Stump (2010, 5–8).

7 Some who work on evil have argued, for different reasons, that we dispense with the term "evil" entirely. See, for example, Cole (2006).

8 This serves as part of Calder's summary of Laurence Thomas's (1993) view, but Calder also notes he is in agreement with this part of Thomas.

9 For an argument against treating the two separately, see Trakakis (2005). In her masterful *Wandering in the Darkness*, Eleonore Stump uses "the problem of suffering" instead of the problem of evil because, regardless of the cause, it is suffering that really concerns us (2010, 4). While I am sympathetic to such an approach, it still may lead one to expect a single solution to both causes of suffering.

1

Evil and Agent-Causal Theism

Richard Brian Davis

That there is evil is evident all around us. Indeed, with the advent of the internet and social media, we're no doubt more aware (painfully so) of the depth and scope of evil than at any other time in human history. However, while evil is confirmed by the facts of experience, it is not always easy to find room for it in our thinking. There is, for example, the claim that evil fits rather badly with theistic ways of thinking—that to believe *There is a God* is contradictory to (or at least strongly disconfirmed by) the belief that there is evil. Substantial philosophical time and resources have been spent on exploring this alleged incongruity. And philosophy, to my mind, is much the better for it. Surprisingly little attention, however, has been paid to the question of whether there might be *other* systems of belief where evil is a bad fit.

In this chapter, I attempt to show that evil exists only if what I call *Agent-Causal Theism* (ACT) is true. According to ACT, human beings are immaterial, conscious agents endued (by God) with a power of self-motion: the power to think, decide, and act for ends in light of reasons, but without being externally caused to do so (even by God himself). By contrast, I argue that there is no space for evil in the worldviews of naturalistic Darwinism or theistic Calvinism.

Making sense of evil

Evil is not hard to recognize. If it were, the so-called problem of evil for theism wouldn't have nearly the psychological force it does. Strangely, however, you can look high and low in that literature and you will scarcely find any account of evil: what it is essentially or how it arose.[1] I recently asked a famous philosopher known for his work on the problem of evil whether in his many travels anyone had ever defined *evil* to his satisfaction. Without a moment's hesitation, he replied "No." I then asked what *he* thought it was. This time there was a pause: "It's enough to say it's 'bad stuff.'"

But *is* that enough? Here we don't need an analytic definition of evil in terms of necessary and sufficient conditions; that would be extremely ambitious given the complex and wide-ranging nature of evil. It will suffice to have a rough-and-ready, working definition: something that gives us a basic grasp (however frail) of the concept, setting the stage for assessing attempts to account for it. To get our bearings, suppose we turn to standard discussions of the problem of evil. Here we meet with the distinction between *moral* and *natural* evil. Moral evil is the evil we normally associate with human choices—for example, to drive a truck into a crowd of innocent people, or to use chemical weapons on one's foes and enemies. Much of the terrible pain human beings (and other sentient animals) have suffered has resulted in this way—at the hands of human beings. But not all of it of course. The religious skeptic is sure to remind us here of natural evils: "A volcano unexpectedly erupts and spills burning lava onto a village; or a tidal wave inundates a coastal town" (Rachels 1991, 105). These are evils the cause of which is purely natural (e.g., plate tectonic movement) and not the result of human (or nonhuman) choice.

Taking the volcano example as a paradigm case gives us something like a *sensation-based* account of evil. According to Epicurus, "All good and evil lies in sensation" (1996, 2). A volcanic eruption in itself is neither good nor evil; it is simply an event that happens. It is only when it leads to pain and suffering on the part of the villagers (or sentient nonhuman animals) that we're at all inclined to call the eruption a natural evil. On the other hand, restricting our attention to cases of human wickedness suggests a *subject-based* account of evil. The most familiar cases of evil, of course, involve human decisions (e.g., Truman's decision to drop the atomic bombs) and actions (e.g., the Boston Marathon bombing). And while these evils are often associated with painful sensations, they aren't constituted by them. This is evident from the fact that there are evils that lack (or could lack) this association. For example, there are thoughts, intentions, and desires that may never be acted upon, may never terminate in painful sensations, but are nevertheless evil—and intrinsically so.[2] But if so, evil cannot *lie* in sensation. Instead, it is plausibly thought to be bound up with a "failure to perform some duty" or "to exhibit some crucial virtue" (Nelson 1991, 370).

Now let's say this is right or at least nearly so. The question then arises: is evil, then, simply wrongdoing? According to Calder (2013), there is a crucial difference. Evil isn't just a matter of going very wrong, or piling up moral wrongs until some threshold for evil is reached. Paradigm cases of evil point to an *inexcusable intent* to bring about or permit *significant harm* when it is within one's power to do otherwise. If a significant harm is one that "a normal rational human being would take considerable pains to avoid" (Calder 2013, 188), Epicurus's painful sensations are certainly in view even if they don't define evil. What evil involves—essentially and at its core—is an immoral thought, desire, decision, or action (freely) entertained or undertaken by a conscious, rational agent to deliberately cause or permit significant harm to be done to herself or others for the sake of an unjustifiable end.

This partial sketch captures the notion I have in mind, and while there is need for more chisholming (when isn't there?), it will be adequate for present purposes. The thing to see is that if this is even approximately what evil comes to, the only worldviews capable of accommodating the reality of evil will be those that can make room for conscious agents with the power to think, desire, decide, and act freely. In what follows, and solely for the sake of convenience, I shall carry out my discussion of ACT and its rivals primarily in terms of our decisions and actions with the proviso that thoughts, desires, and intents are equally in view.

Making space for evil

The freedom condition

Thus, a staff moves a stone, and is moved by a hand, which is
moved by a man.

— ARISTOTLE

To do something evil is to do something for which one is guilty,
responsible, and perhaps even subject to punishment. In an ordinary
and straightforward sense, this implies that evil is freely chosen.
According to ACT, to say that I have freely performed an action
means, in the first place, that *I myself* have decided to undertake
it. I am the agent or author of that action: its first mover, so to
speak. Thus, it is my responsibility. Evil results from my misuse of
the power I have of self-motion, of initiating volitions to act—for
example, *making* decisions or *forming* "effective intentions"[3]—in
light of the reasons I have for acting.

Now why think I have this sort of freedom—call it *agent-causal
freedom*? Two reasons. In the first place, it fits in perfectly with the
facts of my experience. At least on some occasions (the ones on which
I take myself to have acted freely), I experience myself as having
decided to act upon one set of reasons when I am perfectly aware
that I could have acted upon another. As Hasker notes, this may
not prove that I have agent-causal freedom, but "it does establish
a powerful presumption in its favor—a presumption that ought to
be overcome only by the strongest possible reasons for the contrary
position" (Hasker 1999, 85). The meager possibility that I am wrong
hardly counts as the strongest possible reason for thinking I am.

Furthermore, if I do not have the power of self-motion, then
my decisions to act (/refrain from acting) have been determined by
a series of prior causes, in which case I am not, strictly speaking,
an agent—that is, the originating cause of my decisions. Rather,
I am a mere patient *acted upon* by necessitating causes. To speak
of "my decision" to do evil in that case is just a façon de parler: a
mere name we give to an effect produced in me by its real author
(something or someone else up the causal chain). In actual fact, the
"decision" isn't mine. It doesn't originate *with* me; it happens *to*
me. However, as Samuel Clarke, the Great Libertarian, points out,

this immediately leads to grief. For it means that I am no more a responsible agent than is a watch or a clock:

> A Necessary Agent or Necessary Action is a Contradiction in Terms. For whatever *acts Necessarily* does not indeed *act at all*, but is only *acted upon*; is not at all an *Agent*, but a mere *Patient*; does not *move*, but is *moved* only. *Clocks* and *watches*, are in no sense *Agents*; neither is their *Motion*, in any sense, an *Action*.[4] (1717, 5)

Thus, no man "can be angry with his clock for going wrong" (Clarke and Collins 2011, 276). And even supposing that a clock were endued (by God) with intelligence and perception, all that would imply is that it had "understanding enough to feel and be sensible that its weights necessitated" (Clarke and Collins 2011) the movement of its hands. It wouldn't indicate that the clock could in any sense be held responsible for those movements.

This raises a related point. The reason we don't blame clocks for their evil doing is that we recognize that they cannot avoid doing what they do. Given the arrangement of their parts, and the laws governing their mechanical interactions, they operate out of sheer necessity. They don't have the power of doing good or evil because they don't have the power to (decide to) do otherwise. Of course, if one of Clarke's sentient clocks (call it "Lumière") could decide to speed up or slow down, Lumière might be praised for having kept the correct time (when it needn't have), and censured when it didn't (but could have), thereby misleading me about the time and making me late for an important meeting with the dean. But if it isn't so much as possible that Lumière fails to operate as it does, then sentient or not, Lumière doesn't mark the time *freely*, and its movements aren't properly classed as good or evil.

But wouldn't the same go for human beings? If it turns out that there are always prior factors determining my actions and decisions, then wouldn't I, too, be incapable of good or evil? To be sure, human beings are vastly more complicated than clocks (even Apple watches). But complexity isn't the issue here. As Derk Pereboom rightly notes, what's at stake is whether we human beings are genuinely free agents:

> I think that if we were undetermined agent-causes—if we as substances had the power to cause decisions without being

causally determined to cause them—we might well then have the sort of free will required for moral responsibility. (2007, 94)

And then we might also have the requisite freedom for doing good or evil. The question is: *do* we have agent-causal freedom? To begin with, we must note that there are certain worldviews that rule this out *a priori*, and therefore on which evil cannot be said to exist.

Darwinian determinism

Consider, first, *Darwinism*—not the biological theory we all know and love, but its naturalistic construal. According to the most prominent and powerful versions of naturalism, there are no immaterial persons: no God or gods, no immaterial souls or selves (angelic or human).[5] If there are any immaterial entities (numbers or sets, let's say), they are wholly abstract, impersonal, and causally effete—untouched by evolutionary forces.[6] That's fair enough. According to Darwinian Naturalism (DN), however, that's not the way things go for us. Human beings are entirely concrete and physical in nature. Thus Churchland:

> The important point about the standard evolutionary story is that the human species and all of its features are the wholly physical outcome of a purely physical process. . . . If this is the correct account of our origins, then there seems neither need, nor room, to fit *any* nonphysical substance or properties into our theoretical account of ourselves. We are creatures of matter. And we should learn to live with that fact. (2013, 35; emphasis added)

Perhaps this is (part of) what Pereboom is driving at when he says that agent-causal freedom, while a "coherent possibility," is simply "not credible given our best physical theories" (2013). If, according to DN, there is no "room" in the world for "any nonphysical substances or properties," then the physical realm— the only realm in which we have any foothold—is causally closed. It follows that everything true of us (e.g., our thinking, deciding, and acting) has been determined by a series of prior physical causes, stretching back to at least Haldane's "hot dilute soup" (1929, 7), which, I assure you, could do none of these things. But then surely it wouldn't be within our power (yours or mine) to think, decide, or act anywise other than we do; in which case we wouldn't be responsible agents, but mere evolutionary Lumières: capable of neither good nor evil; subject to neither praise nor blame.

Now here the Darwinian naturalist is not without reply. According to Michael Ruse, for example, while we must admit that Darwinian mechanisms determine our *general* features, we needn't think of this as robbing us of our *specific* ability "to change, to readjust and to go forward" in our struggle for survival:

> Nature has given our brains certain genetically determined, strategic rules or directives. . . . Rather like a self-correcting machine, let us say Mars Rover, which can adjust its direction and go around large rocks and so forth (without direction from Mother Earth), so we humans can adjust and go in different directions when faced with different obstacles to our well-being. The rules are fixed, but how we use the rules is not. (2012b, 60)

So the idea, I take it, is that just as the Mars Rover can make autonomous course corrections ("without direction from Mother Earth"), we too can decide to adjust the course of our lives in "different directions," thereby establishing that we *can* do otherwise even within a Darwinian framework. We're causally determined to *make course corrections*, but not to take *this* or *that* course. That is up to us. *We* make the mid-course adjustments.

Now Ruse's argument is an analogy: a likening of self-determining (human) agents to self-driving machines. This naturally raises the question: just how similar are these things in the relevant respects? Simply noting the fact that the Mars Rover can "adjust its direction" doesn't even begin to show that (like us) it can be held responsible for its actions or decisions. And it's not difficult to see why.

A self-driving vehicle, like the Mars Rover, operates by way of a complex system of cameras and sensors. These function to detect the movement and position of nearby objects, and then transmit that data to an onboard computer hardwired up front with fixed "rules"—for example:

CLIFF AHEAD: If there is a cliff ahead, apply maximum pressure to the brakes.

Now let's dub the computer (likely some Apple product or another) "iOS." It is important to see that iOS doesn't *decide* whether or even how a rule like CLIFF AHEAD is used. *Whether* it is used on a given occasion depends on its antecedent being satisfied: a condition that will be met only if *there is* a cliff ahead or not. But surely *that* isn't the sort of thing that is decided by the Rover's iOS—not unless it happens to be outfitted with Kant's twelve categories of the understanding! *How* it is used is settled solely by its consequent. Upon receiving "cliff ahead" data, iOS has no choice about whether to brake. It therefore lacks the freedom we ordinarily associate with being responsible for what one does. The fact is iOS is little more than Lumière without the sentience. The application to the human iOS (i.e., our brains) is patent.

There is a further difficulty. If our brains operate in similar fashion, we cannot censure the degenerate thinking that so often motivates evil activities. Consider a simple example. Just prior to Vladimir Putin's signing into law a new measure decriminalizing some forms of domestic violence (including wife-beating), the Russian paper *Komsomolskaya Pravda* ran a piece defending the move.[7] Appealing to the findings of evolutionary psychologist Satoshi Kanazawa, the author of the article reasoned as follows:

p: Women subjected to non-lethal domestic abuse have an increased likelihood of giving birth to boys.

Therefore,

q: We need to pass a law decriminalizing non-lethal domestic abuse.

Now let's suppose that this represents the actual line of thinking Putin relied upon in coming to his decision—a decision we all recognize as plainly and appallingly evil.[8] It is natural to think that Putin was responsible not only for the decision, but also the thinking that fueled it.

But is that something Ruse can affirm? I doubt it. Let "$T(p)$" and "$T(q)$" stand for "Putin's thought that p,"[9] and "Putin's thought that q," respectively. Then consider the transition from $T(p)$ to $T(q)$. What explains that? The obvious initial reply is:

ANSWER: $T(q)$ obtains because $T(p)$ obtains.

However, there is a subtle ambiguity in the word "because" here.[10] Does it indicate the relation of cause-effect (e.g., "Blood circulates because the heart pumps") or ground-consequent (e.g., "Isaac thinks that gravity has a cause because he thinks it is a force")?[11] Construed in the first way, what ANSWER tells us is that

ANSWER$_1$: $T(q)$ has been caused by $T(p)$.

But ANSWER can also be taken to express a movement in our thinking from a rational ground to a consequent. That gives us a vastly different reading:

ANSWER$_2$: $T(q)$ has been inferred from $T(p)$.

Now the thing to see is that these two answers run at cross-purposes. Intuitively, ANSWER$_2$ will be an inference for which Putin can be praised or blamed only if he could have refrained from $T(q)$ given $T(p)$. The failure here isn't simply logical or epistemic; given the stakes, it is also a moral failing. But on DN, I take it, ANSWER$_1$ is axiomatic: $T(p)$ and $T(q)$ are physical event-structures in Putin's brain; and then if Ruse is right, these are related as Cause and Effect by "genetically determined, strategic rules or directives."[12] Not only is $T(q)$ caused by $T(p)$, $T(p)$ is itself the final link in a chain of prior Darwinian causes. It's determinism all the way down.

Someone might object that Putin certainly is responsible for his musings on domestic abuse. For we can easily imagine him refraining from $T(q)$ under a different set of circumstances, perhaps even embracing $T(\text{not-}q)$. But here there is confusion. The question isn't whether Putin could have failed to think q, if instead of thinking p he had been caused to think some *other* proposition. That is possible but presently irrelevant. It only means that Putin's "refraining" isn't free, and thus not something for which we're inclined to give him credit. The salient question lies in a different direction: can Putin refrain from (thinking q while being caused [by thinking p] to think q)? And the answer, on DN, seems perfectly clear: he cannot.

The problem here, fundamentally, is that DN fails to respect the basic distinction between *drawing* a conclusion (for which one can be appraised) and being *determined* to hold it (for which one cannot). These are decidedly not the same. Indeed, as we all know, the right use of our reason in distinguishing good from evil (and acting accordingly) requires that we routinely exercise our power to resist certain inferences.[13] Unfortunately, if the universe is causally closed, and if our thoughts *just are* physical event-causes, this is a power we do not possess.

Divine determinism

At this juncture, it is tempting to think that moving to an open universe (say, a theistic one) might greatly improve our chances of securing the freedom necessary to account for evil's coming to be. The temptation must be resisted—at least in certain respects. For there are varieties of theism every bit as deterministic (and hence evil-negating) as the Darwinian worlds of Ruse, Sagan, and Dawkins. I'm thinking, of course, of Calvinistic Theism, according to which everything that occurs in human history down to the smallest detail (including all the evil there is) is ordained by God.

Now it seems to me that as far as freedom and moral responsibility are concerned, Calvinism is no less unlovely than naturalistic Darwinism. Thus, for example, Calvin declares of God: "His will is, and rightly ought to be, the cause of *all* things that are . . . it pertains to his might to rule and control everything by his hand" ([1559] 1960, 949, 956; emphasis added). How is it that everything occurs according to the set purpose and foreknowledge of God? Calvin's answer, apparently, is that God causes everything: every human thought, desire, decision, and action. He knows and is in control of these things because (directly or indirectly) he is the cause of them.

There are obvious problems here. If God's will is "the cause of all things that are," then undoubtedly God is the author of evil—a welcome conclusion no doubt to atheist arguers from evil who have always suspected as much. For if we know anything at all, we know that evil exists. The reply, of course, will be that God doesn't cause these things; he merely *permits* them. There is a difference. Thus, according to the Calvinist philosopher Paul Helm,

[God] positively governs all acts that occur except those which are evil, and he negatively governs evil acts by knowingly and willingly permitting them. . . . However, to knowingly and willingly permit an action is not to cause that action; it is to provide a necessary but not a sufficient causal condition for the action. (2001, 179–80)

Since God only permits the evil act, he isn't culpable for it. The culpability remains with the human agent who is its cause. In principle, I suppose, this is the right thing for the Calvinist to say. Unfortunately, it plays havoc with her system.

Following Helm, let's suppose that God doesn't causally determine everything. The question, in that case, is how God could know and ensure that things unfold according to plan. How is that supposed to work? Helm has a suggestion:

God can only control an evil action . . . by deciding not to prevent it; and the evil action occurs because it is caused by the natures and circumstances of those who perpetrate it, not by God (because God cannot cause it). (2001, 179)

Or again, he says, "human nature being what it is, evil results" (2001, 177). We "have an inclination to evil" (2001). Well, perhaps so; but even if so, that hardly explains how God could know in advance that (say) Judas will betray Christ for *exactly* thirty pieces of silver, as opposed to forty, fifty, or a hundred. How is that *specific* detail supposed to be deduced from the *general* fact that Judas has evil inclinations? Wouldn't that be like trying to figure out what I'll be ordering at dinner tonight from the general fact that I'm hungry? It seems a hopeless business.

In any event, the fact remains that all evil actions are caused: if not by God, then by our natures and circumstances. I doubt Ruse would say much different. Not surprisingly, to secure our responsibility for evil, Helm goes on to prescribe a strong dose of *soft determinism* or *compatibilism*: "The idea that human actions are free in a sense that is consistent with determinism," (2001, 169) and thus "compatible with human moral responsibility" (2010, 116). For although Judas could not have done otherwise under the circumstances, nevertheless he doesn't act contrary to his desires. Judas is therefore both free and responsible.

This is a familiar move, but its attractiveness rather abates once we learn that (on both Calvinism and Darwinism) the evil desire Judas is determined to act upon is one he was determined to have. Hence, if being free means doing what one wants or desires, Judas is free only in the sense that Lumière is. He is subject to his predetermined thoughts and desires in the same way that Lumière is subject to the operation of its weights. He doesn't direct them; they direct him. We can call this freedom if we like, but giving it that *name* won't make Judas responsible for his actions. Indeed, if this is what freedom is, I think we have a good reason for drawing precisely the opposite conclusion: Judas is guilty of neither wrongdoing nor evil.

But let us waive these points, assuming for argument's sake that compatibilism is true. How does that help? Compatibilism can only play its role if there is evil. But that is a rather big *if*, I think, for the likes of Helm and Ruse. Here each faces a daunting *origin problem*. For Helm's part, he recognizes that there is "the unresolved problem of the entry of evil into a universe created good . . . and exactly how evil comes about in a world created by an all-good God" (2001, 178–79). For Calvinism, however, the problem isn't only unresolved; it is unresolvable. This is because of its twin commitments to:

C1: Evil is the effect of an evil-inclining human nature

and

C2: Evil-inclining human natures are an effect of "the Fall."[14]

The expression "the Fall" refers to a free and deliberate choice to disobey God made by those human beings originally created by God. (Call this choice DISOBEY.) We can think of DISOBEY as the "original sin" or first evil so to speak.

Now C1 and C2 are incompatible: if either is true, the other is not. Let "EN" stand for the first evil-inclining nature. According to C1, DISOBEY is caused by EN. According to C2, DISOBEY causes EN. So we have a cart before (and after) the horse problem. Moreover, cleaving to C1 leads to a fatal dilemma. Note first that if EN causes DISOBEY, but God is the cause of EN (in virtue of his creating human beings), then God is the cause of DISOBEY,[15] and thus the originating cause of evil.

Understandably, Helm rejects this alternative. What then *is* the cause of DISOBEY? If it isn't the human agent exercising her power of self-motion (i.e., to decide to act, but without being caused to do so), then the efficient cause of DISOBEY must either be the agent's nature, circumstances, or reasons for acting. But it can't be her nature[16] or circumstances, since (by hypothesis) everything was "created good." Nor can it be her arguments, reasons, or motives for acting; for these are abstract considerations at best. They aren't (and cannot be) efficient causes of action.

It follows that it is the agent herself who brings about DISOBEY. She decides to DISOBEY in light of the reasons she possesses. But those reasons don't cause DISOBEY; they merely occasion and inform it. The upshot for Helm is this: if C1 is true, then either God is the agent-cause of evil or human beings are. Since Helm agrees that God isn't, he is committed to saying human agents are. In a strange twist, then, the first and paradigm case of a free choice to do evil supports ACT (over Helm's Calvinism). For consistency's sake, therefore, I heartily recommend it to him.

Ruse is another matter. He faces a different (thankfully shorter) dilemma. On the sensation or subject-based accounts of evil, there cannot be evil unless there are conscious agents. But on Darwinian Naturalism, whence come these agents with the power to think, decide, and act? Helm at least can appeal to a Supreme immaterial, conscious agent (God) as the cause of these powers. What can Ruse appeal to?

The consciousness condition

Intelligence is not figure and consciousness is not motion.

— SAMUEL CLARKE

Suppose the universe originally consisted of nothing but matter in motion. Could a being such as myself, a being endowed with consciousness, have ever arisen from such a Democritean state of affairs? What I propose to argue briefly is that it couldn't.[17] I'll conduct the argument in terms of my own consciousness, which I'll name "C." (You shall have to make the application to yourself.) Now C is not the property *being conscious*; it is a trope, as philosophers like to say: *my* concrete instantiation of *being conscious*. Following Clarke, think of C as the introspective act "by which I know that I think, and that my thought and actions are my own and not another's" (Clarke and Collins 2011, 90).[18] As far as experience goes, C presents itself to me as single (it is *one* consciousness) and unified (it has no parts).

And now let's suppose, following DN, that I am identical with my brain ("B" for short), consisting of parts $p_1, p_2, \ldots p_n$. Like any material system, B *just is* the sum of its parts; it isn't one more thing beyond that collection of parts. Hasker puts it nicely:

> The brain as a whole is not an *additional* concrete object over and above its parts, any more than, in Gilbert Ryle's example, Oxford University is an additional object over and above the colleges, libraries, and so on of which it consists. (1999, 139)

But then for C to inhere in (/belong to) B is just for it to inhere in $<p_1, p_2, \ldots p_n>$. But surely this is absurd. For it implies either that

(1) Each part of $<p_1, p_2, \ldots p_n>$ has C—that is, p_1 has C, p_2 has C, $\ldots p_n$ has C;

or

(2) Each part of $<p_1, p_2, \ldots p_n>$ has a part of C, with C consisting in the aggregate of these partial consciousnesses.[19]

Here (1) and (2) are beset by similar problems. First of all, there is a *panpsychism problem*; they are both committed to the wholly incredible thesis that each and every part of my brain (however minute) is conscious! Secondly, there is a *composition problem*. My consciousness, C, is single and undivided; however, an aggregate of distinct consciousnesses is not.[20] When you compound distinct parts you get a complex (not a unified) whole. It won't help to say that these multiple consciousnesses are unified "if there is something it is like for a subject to be in [these] states simultaneously" (Bayne and Chalmers 2003, 32). For here there is no single subject that has (and thus unifies) this multitude. Our subject is B, a material aggregate composed of a dizzying number of definite and discrete parts. And, I'm sorry to say, it is a composition fallacy to argue that since each of these parts is conscious or quasi-conscious, there is something it is like for B (that compound whole) to be conscious.

But all of this is too easy, you say. No Darwinian materialist thinks the parts of the brain are conscious or partially conscious. Of course not. Rather, the thinking is this: the properties of, and relations between B's parts, taken together, somehow generate consciousness at the level of the material whole (B itself). Let "$R[p_1, p_2, \ldots p_n]$" stand for that relational complex. The claim, then, is that $R[p_1, p_2, \ldots p_n]$ causes C to inhere in B even though the parts of my brain are utterly void of consciousness. Is that a plausible suggestion? Well, I don't think so.

The problem is essentially *categorial*. Samuel Clarke, the Great Newtonian, puts it this way. Take all the powers and properties of a material system that you please, and then unite them "in one operation or power to operate" (Clarke and Collins 2011, 94). This may well result in the material compound's having a different power or property than those found "in the particles singly considered" (as, for example, when "two triangles put together make a square" (Clarke [1705] 1998, 42). But it will always be *of the same species*— say, another geometrical figure. Yet he says,

> Those [same] powers cannot, without an evident contradiction, be the cause of the existence of any other power of a *different species* (as *thinking* is confessedly of a *different species* from *magnitude*, *figure*, *motion* or whatever other properties may belong to *unthinking* particles of matter). (Clarke and Collins 2011, 94)

We are given the effect by hypothesis. My brain is conscious. But if that is the effect, what is its cause? Since the brain is nothing but the sum of its parts, to get consciousness at the compound level, it must be "built up" out of those parts (and their properties). But therein lies the problem. For thinking and consciousness are "the farthest distant from the known properties of matter" (Clarke [1705] 1998, 57). They are radically categorially distinct. You might as well argue that we could get a flavor or a color by adding 7 and 5. So we have an effect (that which is caused), but no properly outfitted cause to produce that effect. This isn't just "magic" (as Nagel suggests (2012, 56); it's getting something from nothing—a plain contradiction.[21]

The upshot is that my thinking or consciousness cannot reside in my brain, or for that matter any material object composed of parts.

Darwinian mechanisms, as wonderfully creative as they are at the biological level, can never generate consciousness or thinking of the sort that would make evil even a possibility. The conclusion to be drawn (since I am conscious) is that my consciousness resides in an undivided, immaterial substance. However, with naturalism out of the picture, we're left with only two possible explanations of this fact. My consciousness has either been communicated to me via an endless series of conscious dependent beings (an ESCDB), not terminating in Haldane's unconscious soup; or it has been produced in me by an immaterial, conscious Supreme Agent (i.e., God). But the former collapses into the latter here, since the cause or reason of an ESCDB must lie outside that series. For, by definition, no member of an ESCDB—hence the series itself—exists by a necessity of its own nature. The cause of my consciousness (and, by extension, my powers of thinking and agency) is therefore to be found in the divine will.

Conclusion

That there is evil is undeniable. The question is how to account for it. And the fact is: not all worldviews can. If evil resides in sensation, as Epicurus tells us, then to account for evil requires that we account for consciousness—something without which there couldn't be pain or suffering. If we opt for a subject-based account of evil, things only get more difficult. For then we have the additional chore of explaining how there could be evil if conscious agents lack the power to author (/originate) their actions or decisions for the sake of ends and in light of reasons. Darwinian Naturalism and Calvinistic Theism rob us of this power. Hence, they evacuate the world of evil, or perhaps (as on Calvinism) locate its origins in God.

By contrast, ACT faces none of these obstacles. It provides an intuitive, principled basis for claiming that evil and the responsibility for it reside in the power of conscious human agents to freely originate thoughts, decisions, and actions which might well (if that power is misused) bring about evil. But neither you nor I would have this power in the first place, if there weren't an immaterial, conscious Supreme Agent. Ironically, then, evil can only exist if God does. So he does.[22]

Notes

1 A notable exception is Mark Nelson (1991).

2 To underscore this point, a proponent of ACT might appeal not only to her own introspective experience, but also prior tradition: "For out of the heart come evil thoughts, murder, adultery, sexual immorality, theft, false witness, slander" (Mt. 15:19, ESV).

3 This is Hasker's term of art, referring to "a state of mind which, in the normal course of events, flows naturally into the intended action; no further deliberation is required" (1999, 88).

4 Compare Thomas Nagel: "There seems no room for agency in a world of neural impulses, chemical reactions, and bone and muscle movements. Even if we add sensation, perceptions, and feelings we don't get action, or doing—there is only what happens" (1986, 111).

5 There are some (very few) naturalists who subscribe to naturalism *light*: the view that although atheism is true, it doesn't follow that we aren't immaterial souls. Compare J. M. E. McTaggart: "Now there is a very common idea that an atheist must either be a materialist or a sceptic. . . . But this, like many other common ideas, is erroneous" (1906, 279). Surprisingly, McTaggart offers no argument at all for this startling assertion.

6 According to Gottlob Frege, for example, if the *truth* of mathematical propositions is a product of evolution, then "it might even be that $2 \times 2 = 4$ itself is destined . . . to develop into $2 \times 2 = 3$!" ([1884] 1980, vi–vii).

7 For details, see Embury-Dennis (2017).

8 It was sure to increase violence against women. Moreover, the justification for (knowingly) allowing these significant harms was inexcusable: the mere desire for more male babies.

9 Following Wielenberg (2008, 95), I take the locution 'S's thought that p' to include S's "conscious endorsement" of p.

10 Noted by C. S. Lewis in his chapter "The Cardinal Difficulty of Naturalism" (1960, 19). For helpful reflections on Lewis here, see Wielenberg (2008, 94–96). See also Victor Reppert (2009, 356–58).

11 Just to be clear: what is in view here is an inferential movement in thinking. We are not talking about the static (platonic) relation of *logical entailment* that necessarily obtains between the premises and conclusion of valid arguments.

12 The point I am making here is not the one frequently imputed to C. S. Lewis, namely, that one thought cannot simultaneously

both *cause* and *entail* another. This point has been challenged by
Lewis's critics. See, for example, Wielenberg (2008, 95); and Peter
van Inwagen (2013). It seems to me, however, that Lewis's point
holds if (following DN) we take thoughts to be physical event-
structures in the brain. On this point, see Paul M. Gould and
Richard Brian Davis (2014).

13 See Isaac Watts ([1792] 1996) for a discussion of the various
    temptations to rash judgment that must be resisted. These include
    (but are not limited to) prejudice, overindulged passions and
    appetites, and the fear of cultural disapproval.

14 See Helm (2001, 177).

15 This follows by the transitivity of causation: A causes B; B causes C;
    therefore, A causes C.

16 Or anything following from her nature—for example, impulses or
    desires to act.

17 The argument I present here is by no means original. It traces back to
    Leibniz (a single paragraph in his *Monadology* §17) and also Kant (a
    slighter longer paragraph in the Second Antinomy). It was also defended
    at length and in great detail by Samuel Clarke. See, for example, his
    correspondence with Anthony Collins (Clarke and Collins 2011). For a
    recent semi-technical formulation, see Hasker (1999, 122–46).

18 In a looser sense, "consciousness" also refers to "the direct act of
    thinking, or the power or capacity of thinking . . . or the power of
    self-motion or beginning motion by the will" (Clarke and Collins
    2011, 108).

19 "Partial consciousnesses": in terms of their scope, not their degree of
    consciousness.

20 Objection: "You say that the consciousness of the parts is distinct
    from C. But on (1) that isn't true. Each part of B has C." Reply:
    consider the property *being my consciousness* or *being C*. Each
    instancing of *being C* by the separate and distinct parts of B will
    count as a separate and distinct trope. This is yet another reason
    for thinking B's parts cannot have C. For if they could, then C (that
    single trope) could be identical with a host of numerically distinct
    consciousness tropes, namely, those of $p_1, p_2, \ldots p_n$.

21 This same basic difficulty plagues Hasker's valiant attempt to generate
    an emergent (immaterial) self or substance (i.e., a "soul-field" as he
    calls it) from $R[p_1, p_2, \ldots p_n]$, and then to attribute my consciousness
    to my soul-field rather than my brain. See Hasker (1999, 188–203).

22 Special thanks to Paul M. Gould and R. Keith Loftin for helpful
    comments and unflagging encouragement.

Response to Richard Brian Davis

Paul Helm

Davis takes a relaxed attitude on how to characterize moral evil, a variegated phenomenon that is impossible to identify in terms of necessary and sufficient conditions. Perhaps it is a case of a Wittgensteinian "family resemblance," which seems to have gone out of fashion. Some cases of moral evil are hard to pin down. So he favors a kind of ostensive approach to identifying acts of evil. Which is fair enough, though it underplays or neglects the fact that in our pluralistic societies there are sharply different views on the shape of evils, though with some overlapping, no doubt. But he is clear on one thing, that the key to the explanation of evil is human freedom understood indeterministically, a phenomenon of the immaterial consciousness and of its powers of agent-causation.

Davis goes into some detail about agent-causation as a version of indeterminism. Let us follow him. Is agent-causal action sufficient for the blameworthy choice of evils? It would seem not. For the occurrence of what is taken to be, and excused from being, moral evil depends on a factor which Davis does not mention, namely, on a human nature which possesses various preferences or proclivities or weaknesses for evil. Why is evil a universal phenomenon, and certain activities evil and not others?

> Man hands on misery to man.
>   It deepens like a coastal shelf.
> Get out as early as you can,
>   And don't have any kids yourself.

> (PHILIP LARKIN, "This Be the Verse," stanza 3)

I don't think we can begin to offer explanations of such phenomena without making reference to what are regarded as the strengths and weaknesses of human nature; however they in turn are identified and understood.

This point has largely been missed in current analytic philosophical treatments of human evil in theodicy. Since the development of Alvin Plantinga's "free will defense," and from its success, there is danger in forgetting its scope. It might seem that Plantinga is in the business of providing an account of human nature. For does he not introduce human depravity, namely what he calls transworld depravity (Plantinga 1974a, 49f.)? But such a construct is not a feature of human nature, a general trait, but a possible state of affairs, a necessary part of a *defense* which Plantinga, the author of the modern analytic defense, was at pains to remind us of. It is not offered as an explanation of evil, but it is an exploration of what God and Curley could and couldn't do if Curley suffers from transworld depravity. Rather it is solely concerned with a response to rebutting the charge that if God is omnipotent, God is wholly good, and evil exists, then theism is inconsistent (Plantinga 1974a, 12–13). In his free will defense Plantinga was not in the business of justifying the ways of God to men. He was concerned with the logical status of a deductive argument, hence his keenness and success with identifying *possible* states of affairs which are defeaters of the Mackie-style atheistic challenge.

Nevertheless, a by-product of the free will defense, as it is colloquially referred to, has been to raise the stock of indeterminism. But however high it is raised it is not the only tool offered in mounting a positive explanation of evil. It is easily seen that it is insufficient. Yet, Davis seems to present it as such.

To complete his presentation, Davis's characterization of the opposed view, divine compatibilism, strikes me as being unnecessarily crude. At least, the empirical evidence he cites in favor of the truth of agent-causation is perfectly consistent with compatibilism. For compatibilists note that we have reasons for action, and that fact makes it uncertain to appeal to it to establish "a powerful presumption" in favor of libertarian agent-causation contra William Hasker, on whom Davis leans at this point (14). If that's all there is to agent-causal indeterminism, then a compatibilist can borrow Davis's locution "decided to act upon one set of reasons when I am perfectly aware that I could have acted upon another," (ibid.) with a good conscience. Consider Joe's hesitation over whether to wear his new yellow tie because it is a gift of his aunt who is coming to tea, when he could instead wear his green tie, hanging next to the yellow tie on the rack, because that is his old favorite. This is an account of hesitation in the course of making up one's mind, which fulfills Hasker's condition, while being consistent with compatibilism. Someone who is compatibilistically free may go through stages in which, until he makes up his mind, he is as ignorant of his future as is any open theist who holds that God is ignorant of some libertarian future.

Without argument, the assertion is that for human freedom God must infuse a person with an immaterial consciousness for which agent-causation is a necessary and sufficient feature. But Davis says no more about God and compatibilism than this. I note here two deficiencies.

First, could an agent-causation account of free will, or indeed any indeterministic theory of human agency, explain what is widely understood as the occurrence of moral evil? Could compatibilism? Isn't it likely that an answer to that question needs a narrative which includes an account of human nature, not just a mechanism of choice? Oxygen is necessary for the combustion of the match but there needs also to be something which has the property of flammability and which is combustible. Any old match won't do. Similarly, there has to be an account of choice. A theory may make a case for the possibility of morally evil actions, but more is needed for an explanation of moral goodness and evil than the invocation of such a state of affairs. If we are talking of human choice and moral evil, then there must be something about human beings that makes each one liable to evil courses of action. The bare logical possibility of that won't do, but some propensity or likelihood for evil is needed—either a feature of human nature or of a combination of such a feature plus circumstance. Why is moral evil universal, but falls short of being metaphysically necessary?

And then as a responsible theist Davis needs to provide some account of how that liability comes to be present and how it is superintended by God. This account should be accompanied by some facts or beliefs. This leads us to the second deficiency, as I see things.

Despite entitling his piece "Evil and Agent-Causal Theism," Davis does not say much at all about the theistic side of things, except that God provides the delivery mechanism for the free (indeterministic) occurrence of moral evil when it does occur. That is a pity. All that we are told is that there is or must be a Supreme Agency who is the Creator of immaterial souls. But what character does this supremo possess? Is he benign or malign? Holy or unholy? And it would be good to have answers to such questions and to know about God's knowledge and power. Does he have foreknowledge of what this delivery mechanism, critical for the choice of bringing about evil, namely freely exercised reasons for doing evil, does in fact deliver? Is the supremo at least a bystander to evil? If so, then he shares some of the responsibility for moral evil that occurs. For it can be presumed that God has a reason for the delivery mechanism to take an evil course, if it does in fact take such a course. And there is such a delivery mechanism in operation (he avers), and there are untold instances of such freely undertaken moral evil.

Finally, I ought to say a little about my own views, which Davis refers to several times. Actions have causal explanations at the level of human agency, and God permits them. But his permission is not general in character but particular, covering particular intentions and actions. He knows the nature and opportunities of his human creatures, and permits them, as being a part of a wider set of circumstances. He knows these things, and the roles they play in bringing certain states of affairs to pass as the result of being our omniscient Creator. I recognize that the origin problem, of how evil originates in a world made good by God, remains.

Apparently, a serious difficulty is, so Davis seems to imply, (21) that God could not know such things as Judas betraying Christ for thirty pieces of silver, in advance. Why not? The particularities are known because God knows not simply general facts about his creatures, but the thoughts and intents of the heart.

He knows how Judas will act and how he makes up his mind. The world of theism is not a world of pure physical mechanism. Nor need Judas, having in mind in advance the number thirty. He may not know this in advance. It may come to him as part of him settling his mind. Nevertheless, God may know, aware he is of the smallest detail of his creation.

Michael Ruse

Let me start straight off by saying that as one who was raised a Quaker, I have great sympathy for Richard Brian Davis's thinking about freedom (Ruse 2018). I feel particularly strongly about this in the Christian context. I am certainly Arminian if not Pelagian in wanting people to make their own choices and not have them clouded or in any sense predetermined by Adam, even if he were to exist—which he doesn't. I am very much a Jesus non-Christian rather than a Paul non-Christian. I want to be able to choose—or not—what Jesus demands of us in the Sermon on the Mount. I defer to no one in my admiration for Saint Augustine, but on questions of original sin, he gives me the creeps. He may not have been able to get over his early-days' sex life, but I thank him very much to stay out of mine. If I am going to hell for having sex with a colleague's wife—although I am not sure that Jesus said a lot about philosophy departments in the 1970s—I am going because of what I did, not because Adam couldn't keep his hands off the stolen fruit. (Oh sorry, that was Saint Augustine, wasn't it? I am not sure that one would want to say that Adam stole the fruit. He is in enough trouble as it is.)

The problem is—where do you go from there? It is always important in addressing these sorts of philosophical questions to look at the whole picture. Problems in philosophy are rarely, if ever, solved straight off. It is always a question of balancing the options and taking the best—realists might say taking the least awful. (I feel a bit that way about the body-mind problem.) Let's boil the issue down to two, putting the Calvinists on one side—but not thereby boiling the issue down to a Christian approach or a non-Christian approach (Ruse 2015). On the one hand, you have some kind of "compatibilism." You have determinism but you insist that you also have free will. The opposite of free will is constraint, not determinism. The problem with Calvinism is not determinism but that it is in the constraint business. On the other hand, you have what is known in the trade as "libertarianism"—not the Ayn Rand type, but free of or from the causal nexus. It is the Kantian autonomous position versus the Humean compatibilist position. My colleague's wife and I unexpectedly find ourselves together and safe from prying eyes for an afternoon. We also conveniently have a bed available. Even in the 1970s, I was getting a bit too old for the rug in front of the fire. Do we have sex or not? Yes, we do indeed.

Notice that if I am now outside the causal nexus at this point of the interaction—I assume that I was in the nexus when I opened the bottle of wine, twisting the screw into the cork, and I assume

I am in the nexus when I get my erection (if I am not, then we really are in trouble)—then everything in my past is irrelevant. No causes pushing me one way or the other—no training from my teachers or resentment at the fact that my colleague has already been having it off with my wife. It just happens. The trouble is: that is not decision-making. That is just craziness. Jonathan Edwards is good on these sorts of things.

> And if habits and dispositions themselves are not virtuous or vicious, then neither is the exercise of these dispositions, for such exercise doesn't involve freedom. Consequently, no man is virtuous through having or acting from a good disposition, and no man is vicious through having or acting from a bad disposition. It makes no difference whether the bias or disposition is habitual or not; if it exists only a moment before the act of will that is its effect, it still makes the act necessary. ([1754] 2017, 85)

He goes on:

> Suppose that some act x of the will does not have a cause. This means that x is not connected with and determined by anything that happens before it; in short, x is absolutely contingent. Allowing this to be possible still won't help the Arminians. For if x happened completely contingently, with no cause at all, then no act of the will, no prior act of the soul, was its cause; no determination or choice by the soul had any hand in it. This accidental event x did indeed occur in the will or the soul, but the will or the soul wasn't the cause of it. The will is not active in causing or determining x, but is purely the passive subject of it. ([1754] 2017, 58)

I realize that Edwards is arguing all of this in the cause of Calvinism. But his general philosophical point can be detached from his theological mission.

So, irrespective of God belief, I find myself pushed toward compatibilism because the other option just doesn't work. After all, there is a lot to be said for the points that Edwards is making. I have been a philosophy professor now for over fifty years. I have taught literally thousands of students. I see my mission in moral terms. I am trying to make my students better people by introducing them to some of the great themes of humankind and some of the greatest minds of the past. I want to fill them full of things that will affect—if you like, determine—their decisions and actions. I don't want my students to talk of wops and wogs and yids and worse—as people regularly did when I was a kid in England. And I want them to get credit when they do the right thing. When one of my students, influenced by philosophy, becomes a public defender rather than a tax lawyer, I swell with pride and so should they. Jonathan Edwards again.

> When someone performs good acts of will, if they come from his strong propensity to good and his very powerful love of virtue—these being an approach to moral necessity—common sense says that he is not less but more deserving of love and praise, worthy of greater respect and higher commendation. . . . And, on the other hand, if a man performs evil acts of mind, e.g. acts of pride or malice, from an ingrained and strong habit of or drive towards haughtiness and malice, this source of his conduct makes him not less but more hateful and blameable, more worthy to be detested and condemned. ([1754] 2017, 102)

Well, what about my side, the compatibilist side? I recognize that we are not just machines like Mars Rover—I am not sure about Dan Dennett from whom I got the analogy—but that is the framework in which we must act (Ruse 2017). And, of course, any advertising executive will tell you that we sure are determined, whatever we may think. Why on earth do you think that *amazon.com* is doing so well, if they cannot massage the massive amounts of information that they have about us all and then play upon us to do what they want rather than what we want? Clearly, what makes us different is all of the thought business. Reasons. My hopping into bed with my colleague's wife is not just a matter of hormones rushing through my excited body—not to mention hers—but the thought that this will be a lot of fun, a thought that I very much hope is mutual. And of course the thought that I can get away with it, because everybody thinks that I am already on the way to the epistemology conference. (That is a lie right there, because I have never been to an epistemology conference in my life. I don't think that even the thought of sleeping with my colleague's wife would make me go to one. And that's another lie, right there.)

Surely, we have reached the level of philosophical maturity when we can appreciate that reasons can be causes. We are no longer caught up with all of that Catholic neo-Wittgensteinianism, thinking that reasons take us out of the real world—meaning the natural world. Humans are special. We are different. Although I am not so sure that we are so very different from higher mammals, especially those like apes and canines that are very social. We are 100 percent more sophisticated and powerful than Mars Rover. And I can certainly be judged for drawing a conclusion however determined I am. You are at perfect liberty to say that I was very wrong to sleep with my colleague's wife, no matter how much I had managed to argue myself into a position where I did it—no matter how much I wanted revenge for what he had done to my wife. (More lies. I couldn't care less about my colleague and my wife. It is all about me and his wife.)

So theologically, I am very much on Richard Brian Davis's side. It is just that, philosophically, he is out to lunch. And he can be blamed for it!

Erik J. Wielenberg

Davis offers a clear and carefully argued case for the claim that the existence of evil (understood in a particular way) requires the truth of a certain type of theism, which Davis calls *Agent-Causal Theism*. Since evil of the relevant sort exists, says Davis, it follows that Agent-Causal Theism is true. We have, then, an interesting moral argument for God's existence—an argument that starts with the existence of evil and ends with the existence of a God who has given to human beings, who are immaterial conscious agents, "a power of self-motion" (11). In developing this argument, Davis claims that the existence of evil is incompatible with the truth of two alternatives to Agent-Causal Theism: Darwinian Naturalism, and Calvinistic Theism. Davis focuses on evil that involves "an immoral thought, desire, decision, or action (freely) entertained or undertaken by a conscious, rational agent to deliberately cause or permit significant harm to be done to herself or others for the sake of an unjustifiable end" (13). This sort of evil requires *agent-causal freedom* and *consciousness*; Davis argues that both Darwinian Naturalism and Calvinistic Theism are incompatible with at least one of these and hence are incompatible with evil of the relevant sort. In response, I draw on some work by Timothy O'Connor to sketch a naturalistic view that I think does make room for the existence of evil. Such a view constitutes a fourth option in addition to Agent-Causal Theism, Darwinian Naturalism, and Calvinistic Theism. To the extent that such a view is plausible, it weakens Davis's case that the existence of evil requires the truth of Agent-Causal Theism.

Proponents of agent-causal freedom maintain that there are two fundamentally different types of causation. On the one hand, there is causation between events, as when the falling of one domino causes the falling of a neighboring domino. Call this type of causation "event-causation." On the other hand, there is the causation of an event by an agent or a person rather than by another event; call this type of causation "agent-causation." According to Davis, the occurrence of genuinely free action requires this second type of causation. He says that when he (or anyone) performs a free action, he is "the agent or author of that action: its first mover" (14). On this sort of view, agents freely act *on the basis* of reasons, but the agent's reasons do not *cause* the agent's actions, for if they did then there would be no role for causation by the agent to play, and the act would not be free.

As Davis understands Darwinian Naturalism, it denies the existence of nonphysical substances or properties which means, according to Davis, that everything true of us (e.g., our thinking, deciding, and acting) has "been determined by a series of prior causes" (ibid.). But that line of reasoning overlooks the possibility of a physical substance functioning as an agent-cause. Timothy O'Connor has defended the view that free action and agent-causation does not "require that agents be a kind of substance radically diverse from physical substance" (2000, 73). O'Connor proposes that the ability to function as an agent-cause is an *emergent* property "exemplified by objects or systems that attain the appropriate level and kind of organizational complexity" (2000, 111). Emergent properties, as understood by O'Connor, are "qualitatively new, macro-level" features of the world that are functions of "certain joint causal potentialities of underlying base properties" (2000). O'Connor and Wong explain this idea in greater detail as follows:

An emergent property of type E will appear only in physical systems achieving some specific threshold of organized complexity. From an empirical point of view, this threshold will be arbitrary, one that would not be anticipated by a theorist whose understanding of the world was derived from theories developed entirely from observations of physical systems below the requisite complexity. In optimal circumstances, such a theorist would come to recognize the locally determinative dispositions of basic physical entities. Hidden from his view, however, would be the tendency (had by each of the basic entities) to generate an emergent state. (2005, 664–65)

On this view, then, certain fundamental physical entities possess the tendency to cause the emergent property of possessing agent-causal power to be instantiated; however, this tendency will become actualized and manifest itself only when various fundamental physical entities are combined in just the right way—for example, in a human brain. This is a view that posits free action and agent-causation that originates with physical brains rather than with nonphysical souls. O'Connor also proposes that phenomenal consciousness—the "what it's like" aspect of experience—is an emergent property. In fact, he suggests that "*a* function of biological consciousness, in its specifically human (and probably certain other mammalian) manifestations, is to subserve the . . . agent-causal capacity" (2000, 122). On this view consciousness is a nonphysical, causally efficacious emergent property. The existence of such a property is incompatible with the truth of Darwinian Naturalism as understood by Davis. However, a view according to which consciousness and agent-causal powers emerge from certain sorts of physical systems is a view that need not include the existence of God or nonphysical souls, and so is naturalistic at least to that extent. Furthermore, O'Connor argues that both conscious experience and agent-causal freedom are, as far as we can tell, compatible with "the emerging scientific picture of the world" and are "not at odds with naturalism" (2000, xv). In defense of this claim, O'Connor distinguishes two theses. The first is the Causal Unity of Nature Thesis, according to which any satisfactory account of a macro-level phenomenon (like free will) "must be consistent with the idea that this *macro*-level phenomenon has arisen through entirely natural *micro*physical causal processes and that its existence continues to causally depend on processes of this kind" (O'Connor 2000, 108). The second and stronger thesis is the Micro-Macro Constitution Thesis, according to which all macro-level phenomena are somehow constituted by and are ultimately "nothing over and above a whole bunch of microphysical goings-on" (O'Connor 2000, 109). O'Connor's position is that while the Causal Unity of Nature Thesis is plausible there is no good reason to accept the Micro-Macro Constitution Thesis. O'Connor's ideas therefore point in the direction of a view that we might call *Naturalistic Emergentism*. According to this view, there is no God or nonphysical souls, the Causal Unity of Nature Thesis is true, and agent-causal freedom and phenomenal consciousness are emergent properties of purely physical human beings (and/or their brains). It seems to me that Naturalistic Emergentism constitutes a plausible version of naturalism on which evil as understood by Davis exists. If this is right, then Davis's contention that the existence of evil requires the truth of Agent-Causal Theism is mistaken.

However, Davis presents an interesting argument against the view that the brain has the property of *being conscious*. If this argument succeeds, it makes trouble for Naturalistic Emergentism. Davis's argument takes the form of a dilemma. He says that if the brain possesses the property of being conscious, C, then either (a) each part of the brain possesses C or (b) each part of the brain possesses some (proper) part of C, such that these individual bits of consciousness somehow add up to C in its entirety. Since both (a) and (b) are implausible, the view that the brain possesses C should be rejected (24). Davis recognizes that there is a third option: perhaps the parts of the brain together "somehow generate consciousness at the level of the material whole" (25) without any individual part of the brain possessing consciousness of any kind. Indeed, that is exactly the possibility embraced by O'Connor. Against this possibility, Davis argues that consciousness and physical stuff "are radically categorially distinct" and so it is implausible that the former could emerge from the latter: "You might as well argue that we could get a flavor or a color by adding 7 and 5" (ibid.). I don't feel the force of the intuition that because consciousness and physical stuff are so different, the former could not causally emerge from the latter. Furthermore, the intuition to which Davis appeals here seems very similar to the intuition that physical matter and immaterial souls are too different to affect each other causally—an intuition that Davis plainly doesn't consider to be decisive. If radically different things can causally affect one another, then why couldn't one sort of thing arise from a radically different type of thing? At any rate, I think that Davis overstates matters when he suggests that emergence of consciousness from the brain involves "a plain contradiction" (25). There is no actual contradiction here; at most there is a violation of some allegedly plausible metaphysical principle. So I don't think that Davis's rejection of the emergentist option is decisive.

I can hardly claim to have shown here that O'Connor's emergentist account of freedom and consciousness is correct. My aim instead is to suggest that Naturalistic Emergentism allows for the existence of evil as understood by Davis and that it is worth taking seriously. And as long as a view like Naturalistic Emergentism remains plausible, Davis has not established his conclusion that "evil can only exist if God does" (26).

Reply to Critics

Richard Brian Davis

I am delighted to reply to Paul Helm, Michael Ruse, and Erik J. Wielenberg. Their challenging comments have given me much to think about, but not (I believe) anything substantial to repent of. In what follows, I take up some of the more pressing issues.

Paul Helm

Paul Helm's comments fall roughly into two parts. First, there is the claim that, as far as explaining evil goes, my Agent-Causal Theism (ACT) is theoretically deficient. It lacks an "account of choice" (31), and it isn't responsibly theistic. Secondly, Helm claims that his brand of theistic determinism is "perfectly consistent" with the "empirical evidence" (30) I cite in favor of agent-causal freedom (apart from which, I say, evil cannot arise).

Let's examine these claims in turn. Note first that ACT involves both an account of evil and of choice. It says, first of all, that a thought, desire, decision, or action (TDDA) counts as evil just in case it is (1) immoral, and (2) freely and deliberately entertained or undertaken, in order to (3) cause or permit significant harm to be done to oneself or others for an unjustifiable end. Thus, contra Helm, I don't think evil "is impossible to identify in terms of necessary and sufficient conditions" (29). I give the conditions—albeit tentatively.

So that's my aerial view of evil. Appended to it is also an account of (free) choice. I say that a TDDA is freely entertained or undertaken only if I am its author or originating cause. I produce it in light of my reasons for doing so. If the cause of my TDDA is something *besides me*—say, some prior determining cause acting upon me to necessitate that thought, desire, decision, or action—then I am an agent in name only; I am Clarke's sentient clock (Lumière): capable of neither good nor evil.

Now according to Helm, in saying all this, I haven't actually given an "account of choice." But why not? What, precisely, is it to do *that*? I must provide a narrative, he says, explaining the universal human "propensity or likelihood" to evil. "If we are talking of human choice and moral evil," this must be cashed out either in terms of "something about human beings that *makes* each one liable to evil," namely, some "feature of human nature, or of a combination of such a feature plus circumstance" (31; emphasis added).

I have two comments. First, if this is what an "account of choice" comes to, Helm is in big conceptual trouble. For then he can account for the blameworthiness of DISOBEY—that original choice to disobey God—only by appeal to the natures and circumstances of those original humans. But then if God is responsible for *that* arrangement, as Helm and I agree, things weren't in fact "created good" and we have every reason to believe that God is the author of evil.

Second, Helm's requested narrative confuses the question of evil's *origin* (How does it arise?) with its *scope* ("Why is evil a universal phenomenon?" (29)). That my account of choice doesn't address the scope question is no reason to think it doesn't answer the origin question. In any event, if an explanation for evil's scope is needed, the proponent of ACT could always adopt an ancillary hypothesis like (C2) above: that evil-inclining human natures are an effect of "the Fall." That would do the trick nicely. The point is that ancillary questions of this sort can be handled by ancillary hypotheses. The same thing goes, I submit, for Helm's faulting ACT for failing to tell us what God is like, or why he bestows agent-causal freedom upon us, knowing that we will misuse it and bring about evil.

Turning to Helm's theistic determinism: while for the most part neglecting my criticisms, he still wants to say that his position is more resilient than I make out. For one thing, it "is perfectly consistent with" (30) the evidence I cite in favor of (the presumption of) our having agent-causal freedom. For a compatibilist can also say that in making a decision she takes to be free, she experiences herself as deciding to act on one set of reasons, while being aware that she is perfectly able *on that very occasion* to act upon another.

Now Helm thinks that the compatibilist can agree to this "with a good conscience" (30–31). But is that really true? I don't think so. Granted: she would have been able to decide to act on those different reasons, if she had been determined to do so by a *different* set of causes (on what would then have been some *other* occasion). But this is strictly beside the point. What I'm talking about is our being aware that we could have decided to act on those different reasons under the *same* causes on *one and the same* occasion. If Helm thinks he has experiences like that, he should dismiss them as illusory (given his theory), or admit there is presumptive evidence for agent-causal freedom and against his determinism.

Michael Ruse

Michael Ruse's comments begin on a happy note ("I have great sympathy for Richard Brian Davis's thinking about freedom" (32–33)), but then sadly take a precipitous turn to his final conclusion: "Philosophically, he is out to lunch" (36). Ruse proceeds mainly by way of story and assertion. Still, I think we can piece together a kind of argument.

An evil TDDA, I argued, must be one that is *freely* entertained or undertaken. Now this creates a severe problem for what Ruse calls in his own chapter "the supreme theory" (92): his Darwinian Naturalism (DN). For on DN, Ruse's decision to have that adulterous affair with his colleague's wife was no more than a physical event-structure in his brain, governed perhaps by "certain genetically determined, strategic rules or directives" (Ruse 2012b, 60). In fact, *he* didn't make that "decision"; it's something that happened *to* him—the inevitable outcome of a chain of prior determining causes and effects. He could no more have refrained from his "choice" than Lumière could have decided to stop its hands from moving. Not only was it not a *free* decision, it wasn't a decision at all. But in that case, it seems to me, Ruse is in the clear. He shouldn't reproach his 1970s self. What he did was neither blameworthy nor evil.

For as Clarke says, no man "can be angry with his clock for going wrong" (2011, 276).

Alas, however, Ruse is made of sterner stuff. What he wants to say, I take it, is that his decision was both determined and free. Like Helm, he finds himself "pushed toward compatibilism" (34). Now why is that? Because, he says, "the other option just doesn't work" (ibid)—that option being the one I defended: agent-causation. The problem seems to be that if I am an agent (or first) cause of an evil choice, then my making that choice is uncaused. But if so, that TDDA occurs for no reason: "It just happens." That "is not decision making," says Ruse. It is "just craziness" (ibid).

I'm afraid this is simply a non sequitur. It is indeed true that if I am the first cause of a TDDA, then nothing is causing me to cause it. It hardly follows that I don't have a reason for causing it. What Ruse is (falsely) assuming here is that reasons are causes, so that if I do something for a reason, that reason is the physical, efficient cause (apparently along with various hormones in Ruse's case) of my doing it. He says we'll come to see this once "we have reached the [appropriate] level of philosophical maturity," where we reject the "thinking that reasons take us out of the real world—meaning the natural world" (36). So there it is. When everything is said and done, the reason to think that reasons are causes is that "the supreme theory" demands it.

But that's not much of a reason. Indeed, it gives rise to a serious category mistake. Reasons are the sorts of things that can serve as premises in arguments. They are *of* or *about* things; brain events and materials (BEMs) are not. Reasons *represent* the world as being this way or that; BEMs do not. Reasons can have a *truth value* and be truth functionally connected (e.g., negated, conjoined, disjoined). Not so for BEMs. Reasons can *logically entail* propositions; BEMs can do no such thing.[1] The fact is: in most crucial respects, reasons are nothing at all like neural event-structures. They aren't physical, efficient causes. Rather, they are abstract final causes that occasion and inform our decisions and actions.

According to Ruse, what "makes us different" from Lumière and the Mars Rover is "all of the thought business. Reasons." Thus "I can certainly be judged for drawing a conclusion however determined I am" (ibid.). But how does that follow? If reasons are physical bits of (brain) hardware, subject to prior necessitating causes and operating according to "genetically determined" directives, we can hardly deny that the Rover also acts on reasons. But then if our reasoning can be judged morally good or evil, so can the Rover's. Nothing could be more absurd.

Sometimes we have to stand up to our cherished theories—at least in certain respects. I would suggest that for Ruse and his all-purpose "supreme theory," that time has come.

Erik J. Wielenberg

I turn finally to Erik J. Wielenberg's challenging and inventive remarks. Wielenberg doesn't dispute my claim that evil TDDAs require agent-causal freedom and consciousness. Nor does he disagree that the existence of evil is incompatible with both Darwinian Naturalism (as I defined it) and Calvinistic Theism. But he thinks I have overlooked "a fourth option" which he styles *Naturalistic Emergentism* (NE)—in brief, a naturalized version of ACT. "To the extent that such a view is plausible," we're told, "it weakens Davis's case that the existence of evil requires the truth of Agent-Causal Theism" (37).

Well, to what extent *is* it plausible? Answer: to the same extent that it is plausible to claim that a material substance can be an agent-cause. This claim constitutes the beating heart of NE. In defense of NE's plausibility, Wielenberg draws upon Timothy O'Connor's work on agent-causation. Remarkably, however, O'Connor himself readily concedes: "Taking the agency theory seriously within a basic materialist framework brings forth a whole host of theoretical problems and issues" (1995, 180). Indeed, it does; here is one such problem.

I defined an agent-cause in terms of the power of self-motion: the power to originate volitions in the light of reasons, but without those reasons or anything else causing one to do so. However, since matter is essentially passive—that is, since it acts only if acted upon—it is conceptually impossible for a material object to be an agent-cause; in which case it is maximally *implausible* to suppose that brains are agent-causes or that they possess agent-causal freedom. Perhaps a case can be mustered up along these lines, but I don't see anything like one (or even the hint of one) in Wielenberg's remarks.

Now what about my other condition for evil: that there be *conscious* agents to bring it about? Here I argued that since consciousness is simple and unified, it cannot belong to a material object composed of parts. Where "B" stands for my brain—a material whole consisting of parts $p_1, p_2, \ldots p_n$—Wielenberg and O'Connor unite as one man to oppose this conclusion. We can consistently affirm, they say, each of the following propositions:

(1) B is identical with the sum of its parts: $p_1, p_2, \ldots p_n$.

(2) B is conscious.

And yet

(3) None of $p_1, p_2, \ldots p_n$ is conscious.

But how is that possible? If (1) is true, B isn't a whole "over and above" $p_1, p_2, \ldots p_n$. It's not a *second* object in addition to those parts. But then surely if (2) is true, (3) is false. For my consciousness to belong to B *just is* for it to belong to $p_1, p_2, \ldots p_n$. So it seems to me that (1)–(3) comprise an inconsistent set.

Wielenberg apparently disagrees. To see that these propositions are consistent, we need only embrace O'Connor's conjecture:

CONJECTURE: Consciousness, though radically categorially distinct from the properties of matter, can be caused to emerge at the macro-level of the brain by the "micro-physical goings-on"[2] of its unconscious parts.

The basic idea, then, is that consciousness is an emergent property of the brain that "*supervenes* on its underlying base properties" (2000, 112)—that is, the properties of $p_1, p_2, \ldots p_n$. O'Connor tells us that consciousness is "simple" or "partless" (2000, 111), and qualifies as a "radically new" feature of the world, "'transcending' the lower level properties from which it emerges" (2000, 112).

CONJECTURE strikes me as a blunt metaphysical impossibility. Let $R[p_1, p_2, \ldots p_n]$ stand for the relational complex consisting of the properties of, and relations between B's parts. Consciousness cannot by *generated by* $R[p_1, p_2, \ldots p_n]$ unless it is in some sense *generated out of* $R[p_1, p_2, \ldots p_n]$. Otherwise, we have a case of something coming to be out of nothing. Wielenberg doesn't "feel the force of the intuition" (39). But it's not clear to me that this is warranted. There are a couple of things to note.

First, although O'Connor speaks of emergent properties as being "exemplified by objects or systems" (2000, 111), this language is apt to be misleading. It suggests that the relationship between my brain and my consciousness is that of exemplification. But it isn't. O'Connor's properties are universals understood as "immanent constituents of the physical world" (2000, 73). They are tropes: concrete, particularized property instances. Now tropes can't be exemplified; that's just a category mistake. Rather, they are *constituents* of their associated objects or systems.[3] So contra O'Connor, the relation obtaining between my consciousness trope (I dubbed it "C") and B is just this: C is a constituent of B. Hence, my brain *does* have conscious parts—precisely the thing CONJECTURE was engineered to avoid.

Secondly, I think O'Connor may well feel the force of the something-from-nothing intuition even if Wielenberg does not. In the end, O'Connor isn't prepared to say that C can be generated *by* R[p_1, p_2, ... p_n] without (in any sense) being generated *out of* it. In terms of "generating an emergent," he says, there is a "tendency, present in each microparticle, to jointly achieve its characteristic effect, which is the generation of a property" (2000, 114). So each of p_1, p_2, ... p_n has an internal *tendency to generate consciousness*. Now if a "tendency to consciousness" is a proto-consciousness, we're saddled with panpsychism. If it isn't a consciousness at all, then what is the plausible story about how such a "tendency" (whatever that means) is grounded in the material properties of the parts of my brain? Here, I'm afraid, we get no answer at all—not even the whisper of a conjecture.

According to Wielenberg, "As long as a view like Naturalistic Emergentism remains plausible, Davis has not established his conclusion that 'evil can only exist if God does'" (40). But that's just it. It isn't plausible.

Notes

1 On these points, see Lewis (1960, 21), Plantinga (1993, 116–17), and Gould and Davis (2014, 52–53).

2 The expression is Timothy O'Connor's. See O'Connor (2000, 109).

3 For details, see Moreland (2013).

2

Evil and Christian Classical Theism

Paul Helm

First, a caveat or two. "Compatibilistic Christianity" is the editor's term for the viewpoint I've agreed to represent. But in considering the matter of explaining evil, mine is not a viewpoint with compatibilism in the major premise. I think that would make it principally a philosophical viewpoint, compatibilism being a philosophical concept. But—I hope—mine is a viewpoint in the faith seeking understanding tradition. It is faith driven, not reason driven. Faith as in "the faith once delivered to the saints" (Jude 3), not as in "Lord, increase our faith" (Lk. 17:5). Just as John Locke wrote of the work of the philosopher as being that of an underlaborer, so it is with philosophy and the Christian faith.

And even when we permit compatibilism in a minor premise we need to remember that it is a twentieth-century word, and so it carries the danger of anachronism when attributing it to earlier thinkers. Not only is compatibilism a philosophical word, it is also by this time ambiguous. Compatibilism can have various connotations, depending on what deterministic factors are said to be consistent with the responsibility of the agent who has them. Thus, there are physical and biological and psychological theories. And the psychological theories may be divided, for example, into monistic and dualistic kinds. So we shall have to work our way to a selection when the time comes. However this may be, I start at a different point than with compatibilism.

The question, "Why evil?" is, for an orthodox (small "o") Christian theist, also significantly ambiguous. An important feature of this contribution to the questions raised by evils is that such a theism is monistic. "All things were made by him; and without him was not any thing made that was made" (Jn 1:3). "Of him, and through him, and to him are all things" (Rom. 11:36). Some contrasting systems are dualistic, positing two equally ultimate sources of good and of evil, Light and Darkness, engaged in an everlasting wrestling match, and so on. Judeo-Christianity is not like this. God is the creator and purposer of all that is. So the question, "Why evil?" when posed of this God, becomes at least two questions.

First, logically and metaphysically, there is the question, "What is God's purpose in permitting/ordaining evil?" The fulfilling of what end or ends required evil? In a world made good by God, indeed, very good, what place does evil serve? This is a question that is teleological in character. I don't think an atheist has a place for this question, because any atheistic system has only one set of sources of evil, namely uncreated matter. A theist may reply to our question by recognizing that he does not have a clue as to why there is evil in God's world. But the question nevertheless makes sense; God must have a ground or grounds. The second question is, "Granted that God is the ordainer of evil, how does evil occur?"

In this monism there are two categories of players: God the creator and human beings his creatures, with the use of their own minds and wills. (And, of course, if we allow the distinction between what is called "natural evil" and "moral evil," the activity of a volcano and that of a thief, say, it may recognize two sorts of evil brought about by created powers.) In materialist atheism, there is only one set of players, configurations of matter more or less complicated. Some of these possess agency, others do not.

In this short piece I shall assume that we may point in the direction of an answer to this question without presuming mastery of detail. Attempting this, the question for the classical Christian theist of why God ordains evil has to do with the purpose or purposes of this God, a pure spirit, of unbounded wisdom and power. If an atheist materialist tries to ask the parallel question, he in effect asks it of the effects of the interactions of matter. Are some of these effects productive of good? This sort of question has a functional cast to it. Do evils foster goods in some or perhaps all cases?

But such questions are not at all like, "Why does God ordain evil?" Rather, for the atheist materialist, this is a question that we, configurations of matter, ask of ourselves and of other configurations of matter. How such configurations get to ask anything is a major problem in such an outlook. Strictly, such grand teleological questions are imputed as *façons de parler* to collocations of material factors and their interactions. Atheists, like theists, may resort to anthropomorphism. Perhaps these evils are bound up with the self-preservation of some species, or of species generally. Maybe evils and pains are spurs to good: to maternal care, or the development of clothing for a covering against heat and cold, or as a sign of the onset of serious sickness. These are areas of very great interest, but they arise from our penchant for imputing functions or purposes to some of the natural order that does not have anything like human intentions as we experience these, and as Christians assign to the creation of human beings, body and soul. And if we are thorough-going materialists, we also have the task of explaining how those arrangements of matter that are you and me come to have the capacity to impute good and evil to other chunks of matter. Good and evil are ultimately epiphenomena of physical changes.

Why does evil occur?

So we now consider the first of the questions that makes sense for a theist, the question of what is the purpose, or are the purposes, to which evil contributes? Of course, evil may have different purposes. Certainly it has different sub-purposes such as the innumerable means that must be achieved to ensure the bringing to pass of the supreme end. But here I shall not give more than a glance at such subordinate means to the grand end.

I take it that an answer to the question of why God created a universe in which there is evil has to do with the achieving of God's purposes. The created universe, whether we think of it as possessing a marvelously intricate physical basis, or within that environment, as including men and women who are created in God's image, or the human race, have as their ends the display of God's power and goodness. "The heavens declare the glory of God" (Ps. 19:1). Of course this scenario will contain actions of human beings that are performed at the behest of human purposes, and we shall make several points about these human goals. All we need to say at present is that these goals may be goals that are in accord with the divine goal, or at variance with it.

So we are in the area of the thought that the universe is arranged for God's good pleasure, or for the display of his perfection. This is of course a position which is found in Scripture, as we have already seen "all things were made by him" (Jn 1:3) and "you created all things, and by your will they existed and were created" (Rev. 4:11). This God-centeredness is characteristic of Christianity in a variety of its forms. However, it is fair to say that in the modern Western world this view is not often given pride of place but is usually displaced by a more or less anthropocentric view of God's purposes. And this is a pity, in my view.

This God-centeredness may have varied forms. In his *Enchiridon,* Augustine affirms that it is "better to bring good out of evil, than not to permit any evil to exist" (1961, ch. 27) and, "nor can we doubt that God does will even in the permission of what is evil. For he permits it only in the justice of His judgment. And surely all that evil as well as good exists, is a good (1961, ch. 96)." And finally, "in a way that is unspeakably strange and wonderful, even what is done in opposition to His will does not defeat His will. For it would not be done did He not permit it (and of course His permission is not unwilling, but willing); nor would a Good Being permit evil to be done only that in his omnipotence He can turn evil into good" (1961, ch. 100). And similarly in Aquinas: "But, as Damascene says, by the mystery of the Incarnation are made known at once the goodness, the wisdom, the justice, and the power or might of God" (*ST* III, Q 1, A 3, s.c.). "And so also the evil of punishment was established by God's justice for God's glory" (*ST* III, Q 1, A 1, ad. 3).

What we have in these words of Augustine and then of Aquinas is an undeveloped form of what came to be called the *felix culpa* defense of evil. In a recent paper Alvin Plantinga recognizes that in drawing attention to this he is in a fashion reinventing the wheel, and that he is considering "a response that has been with us for a long time. I don't claim that this response answers all our questions or relieves all of our perplexity. It does make a contribution along these lines, however" (2004, 5).

In this chapter we have to be content with such a general approach. God is the Lord of good and evil. The good he brings about in varying ways, depending on the good in question; the evil he "willingly permits," as Augustine put it. Sometimes this approach stresses the will of God, as in references to God's "good pleasure"; at other times it stresses God's supremely perfect simple nature that is refracted in the worlds of creation and redemption. In the *felix culpa*, the stress is Christological: if God "spared not his Son, but gave him up for us all" (Rom. 8:32). As space permits, I shall note features of Plantinga's characteristically clear exposition to illustrate this general approach.[1]

Behind this exclamation "*O Felix Culpa*" is the thought that the evil in the world, and especially the evil of the Fall, the "fault," is "happy." Why? Because it made necessary the incarnation, the clothing of God the Son himself with our human nature, body, and soul. He came down, and was incarnate. The fault, the incarnation, and the offering of the Incarnate One is needed, for the display of the glory of God in the redemption of men and women. The point here is not simply that the incarnation was necessary, but that an evil world in which God himself came and suffered for us is incommensurably better than one in which there was no evil, but also that there was no incarnation.

That is, as Plantinga puts it,

> Given the truth of Christian belief, however, there is also a contingent good-making characteristic of our world—one that isn't present in all worlds—that towers enormously above all the rest of the contingent states of affairs included in our world: the unthinkably great good of divine incarnation and atonement. Jesus Christ, the second person of the divine Trinity, incomparably good, holy, and sinless, was willing to empty himself, to take on our flesh and become incarnate, and to suffer and die so that we human beings can have life and be reconciled to the Father. In order to accomplish this, he was willing to undergo suffering of a depth and intensity we cannot so much as imagine, including even the shattering climax of being abandoned by God the Father himself: "My God, my God, why have you forsaken me?" (2004, 7)

Contrast two kinds of possible worlds. In the first kind, there are free creatures who always do only what is right, who live in harmony with God and each other and do so, let's add, through all eternity. Now for each of these worlds W of this kind, there is a world W* of the second kind. In W* God creates the very same creatures as in W, but in W* these free creatures rebel against him, fall into sin and wickedness, turn their backs on God. In W*, however, God graciously provides a means of salvation by way of incarnation and atonement, my claim is that for any worlds W and W*, W* is a better world than W. (2004, 10–11)

So a world including the incarnation of the Son of God is immeasurably better than one without it, since the incarnation involves the humbling of the eternal God for our sakes and for our salvation. As Plantinga notes, this state of affairs entails an incommensurability between such an infinite act of gracious goodness and the finite evils that are permitted in order that God's redemptive powers are displayed and exercised. "It is also incommensurable with creaturely evils, no matter how much sin and suffering and evil that W* contains, it is vastly outweighed by the goodness of God, so that W is a good world, and indeed a very good world" (2004, 9).

This does not mean that the incidence of evil and suffering in this world is not perplexing. It is perplexing partly when it is considered apart from the plan, and because for some the very idea of God having a plan which includes human evil is anathema. Decontextualized it seems unfair, arbitrary, and even devilish, that God should permit evil. But God is Lord of good and evil. For us to consider evil apart from his plan guarantees perplexity.

How does evil occur?

Then there is the question of how? How does evil come to occur? As noted above, there are two questions, the divine end of evil, and the human origin of it. Anyone who endeavors to offer an explanation of evil, say, in terms of physical states, has to end that explanation with the recognition of brute facts. Otherwise the explanation dissolves into an infinite regress. The theist is formally in the same position. He has to end with postulating, say, recherché or otherwise unfamiliar states or events, beyond which it is not possible yet to go further. All explainers of evil are formally in the same boat. The one with a brute physical universe, the other with an appeal to the inscrutable will of God; and if we honor that "not yet" and recognize the need to await more explanations, these, when we have them, will be of the same type, though even more recherché.

If we understand explanation in epistemic terms, as a way of learning, and not as a mere formalism, like the possession by a set of propositions some of which are deducible from others, then at this point for both theist and atheist there is bafflement (Ruben 1990). The theist must end his explanatory narrative by invoking the will of God; it was the good pleasure of God that this is so. Why is it the good pleasure of God that this is so? This is a question that cannot be answered, not because there is no answer, but that there is no answer apart from the will of God. And if the scientific regress is in the hands of an atheist, the explanans also causes bafflement. This does not make these two sorts of regress equivalent, for the theist offers a personal explanation, in terms of divine agency, while the atheist must offer a nonpersonal one, in terms of states and forces.

Given the immaculate and necessary perfection of God, moral evil can only arise from the creature.[2] It is a logical consequence of the monistic character of the Creator-creature distinction that God is the only source of good and that moral evil has its source according to orthodox Christianity in the creature. For the materialist atheist, evil lies in the physical properties, systems, and changes, while for the theist it lies in the immoralities and moral deficiencies of the creature. Goodness has its source in God alone who has fullness of being, and who is alone perfect. Such goodness is conveyed to human agency, which in the ideal case is agency proceeding from an appraisal of the truth and a willingness to carry out the will of God.

Mutability

In the original condition, mankind in the person of Adam was called to obedience, with the possibility of disobedience. Mutability is the condition of possessing a human nature created sinless.

The important consequence of this is that there is about evil a deficiency or loss or negativity. Augustine, influenced somewhat by the neo-platonists at this point, called evil a *privation*. Hence it could not be the direct action of God who is only capable of creating not of destroying. Blindness (say) is not a positive property, but a negative property. Blindness, itself a deficiency, may be a necessary condition of other conditions. It may give rise to the training of guide dogs, or research into the causes of blindness, or in the developing of ingenious skills by the blind to mitigate the effects of this disability. Augustine's gloss of evil as a privation is not altogether fanciful. The Bible says that sin is a "falling short of the glory of God" (Rom. 3:23).

The condition in which humans were first created was unstable, therefore. Creaturely agency is distinct from divine agency. So mankind at the first had instilled in him a good, very good, character. But human agency was such that it was distinct from God's agency. Creation was not immaculate. The possibility of declining was built in. This is not the same view as that propounded by John Hick from Irenaeus; that creation was a form of infantility or immaturity (1966).

Theism is not pantheism. The human beings created by God have minds and wills of their own. So at the first it was mankind that obeyed God, not God that obeyed himself. But humankind was not inalienably good. It was the consequence of a created nature that it was necessarily mutable.[3] Humanity was not created as good as could be, but "very good." People could change for the worse, and they did. The choice was between continuous dependence and willing deviance, knowing the consequence of doing so, but in some fashion also being self-deceived. It is important to stress that such a choice was not a libertarian choice. The original position was not one of neutrality, but that in which human beings were created "very good" by their Creator. It was not that the way of life and the way of death were equidistant or otherwise symmetrically before the chooser. Rather the choice of the way of death was the creature's choice to move away from the original position. So that choice was irrational and rebellious.

In Christianity, evil arises as a decline from the good. In non-theistic systems, evil is a by-product of the functioning of certain individuals within it, a contributor to their development and evolution. How it comes about that the seeds of rebellion were sown in the mind and conscience of the original pair is not clear. Various hypotheses are offered—infancy, inexperience, self-deception, inattention, unbelief, and so on. None of these satisfy, for they all fail to explain satisfactorily how rebellion could take place in a person-created good.

Here is not the place for an at-length treatment of compatibilism, but we may say a word about it. Compatibilism obtains only if human action is both determined and if, under certain conditions, the agent is responsible for what he does or fails to do. It is difficult for some to see how compatibilism can be so without God being the author of sin. It is also difficult for some to see how under compatibilist auspices doing evil can be culpable. This is certainly a problem. But indeterminism also has a problem. I shall make a couple points against the charge that such an arrangement makes God the author of sin, having elsewhere already touched on the primary lure of evil from a theistic point of view (Helm 2015).

First, God is not simply *an* agent, he is *the* agent in the sense that he is the creator ex nihilo of all that is. And not only the creator but also the upholder of what he has initially brought into being, as it develops through time. To call God the primary cause, and his creatures secondary causes, while it makes these points, makes an important equivocation over "cause" as applied to God and to a created agent. The temptation to think of God as a causal agent on a level with human creaturely causal agency must be resisted. As the primary cause God is intimately involved in creating and "upholding" his creatures and all their actions by a kind of *creatio continua*.

A second consideration is that other accounts of human agency have a similar problem. How does the claim that in a world-created good by God, supposing indeterministic choice, such a choice was made to rebel against him? How could that ever become a live option? "To say, the will was self-determined, or determined by free choice, in that sinful volition; which is to say, that the first sinful volition was determined by a foregoing sinful volition; is no solution of the difficulty" (Edwards [1754] 1957, 414).

Here is a good example of recognizing mystery or of confessing necessary ignorance. I guess the reader has already noticed others. The philosopher in us would ferret a reason out or he may alter the premises of the argument of which is the conclusion. But that's not the way of faith seeking understanding. This difficulty is brought about by a factor about God which is largely ignored or forgotten or resisted at present: the idea that God himself has a will— an "agenda"—of his own. God is not passive, nor out to satisfy his creatures' every whim and legitimate aspiration. The Judeo-Christian tradition has a different shape if the idea that God had a will of his own is jettisoned.

However, the onset of evil is to be explained, human beings declining from the original position is in effect an act of rebellion and resistance to their Lord. Mankind having fallen, cannot by his own effort attain to the original position. The Fall is ratchet-like in its effects, in that once chosen, the path cannot be regained. For the original free will does not have mastery over good and evil, but is itself affected by its action. Humankind cannot re-motivate itself in the service and devotion to his Lord. Human beings are wanderers, aliens, rebels.

But this state of affairs, though bad, is not as bad as could be. The Christian, following Scripture, recognizes a place for natural law,[4] the moral sense that has outlasted the collapse of the Fall. The result of the Fall is, logically or metaphysically, an accident. This does not mean that the loss was trivial. What was lost was the image of God, the knowledge of God, and the personal holiness and righteousness that went with it. So it is a profound moral loss. But mankind is not denatured, humans do not become bestial, but retain their human nature, their essence. They can reason, they can set themselves goals, they can interact with their environment, they can investigate, and form social groupings and social goals. They have a sense of mine and yours, of fairness and of fidelity, and so on. Human beings, unlike, say, sheep, have a conscience, a moral sense which they can apply to themselves and to others. So things are not as bad as they could be.

Of course a main task for Christians and anyone else (according to Christian theism) is not simply to try to work out a tolerable understanding of God's relation to the evil (as its source), but at the personal level to attempt to stem and ameliorate conditions which are evil both in himself and herself and in the culture around. Not merely to talk the talk, but walk the walk. There are obvious things that occur in developing such a program, and others less obvious. For example, the Christian does not subscribe to the fashionable doctrine that what matters is one's public life and one's private life is something else. It commends a strong sense of personal integrity.

Then there is the question of consistency. Those who propose to outlaw stealing ought not themselves to steal. And there is the question of the inner self, the character of motivation. Jesus stresses the importance of the heart. As a man thinks in his heart, so is he.

Important as policies of social justice and the amelioration of human conditions are, petitions for the coming of an earthly kingdom, with Jesus as its king are something else. Jesus is clear that his kingdom is not of this world. If it were, then his servants would fight. Since the time of Augustine, if not before, Christians have thought of human life and culture as taking place in two cities or two kingdoms. The city of this world, "Babylon" as the New Testament and Augustine called it, has to do with life together in this passing world, a place of exile. Alongside this city is the City of God, whose citizens have aspirations and a destiny that lies not in the arrival of some earthly Utopia, but in the coming city which has foundations, whose maker and builder is God. This is the new Jerusalem. The kingdom of God is eschatological and final.

In what has gone before I have sketched out a range of matters constitutive of what I have called Christian theism and some of its consequences for good and evil. Christians who hold such views, particular these views of origins, and of the creation— fall—redemption sequence, are aware that they are at odds with (to look no further) the modern scientific view of origins and their evolutionary development, as well as with culture more generally. To look no further, it seems hopeless to map the present scientific account of the emergence of *homo sapiens* with the biblical account of the creation. Modern Christians are acutely aware of the disparity and tension that these two allegiances create. So having spent most of this time with the metaphysics of Christian theism, with these tensions in mind, I turn finally to address epistemological questions, and particularly the presence of epistemic tensions. How are such large-scale tensions to be addressed?

Rational perplexity and belief policies

It is common to think of our beliefs as a spider's web.[5] The more certain the belief, the nearer to the center it is located, the more certain to the person whose web it is. We are supposing here that "certain" is not the name for a feeling merely, something purely or mainly subjective, but it is epistemic in character. That is, it is grounded in some evidence; it has an evidential base, one that is appropriate to the sort of belief that it is. In general where there is less certainty, more movement and change, the nearer the belief is to the periphery. The periphery includes beliefs that change as we live from day to day, and as we think and learn more about them and their grounding. And it also contains longer-term beliefs that are held tentatively, and therefore liable to change. Perhaps such a change means that the position moves to the center, or that it is replaced by an alternative belief in more or less the same place. Like a web, if those strands toward the center are disturbed then the disturbance to the rest of the web will be potentially greater than that made by a disturbance at the periphery. To borrow another epistemological metaphor, the center of the web will be the foundation, consisting of indubitable and other weight-bearing beliefs. The periphery is the superstructure which depends on the foundation.[6]

Now suppose we think not of a web, but of webs in plural. These webs may develop over time as we mature, are educated in a particular way, are influenced in other ways, and so forth. So suppose a web of religious beliefs, one of scientific theories, and one of common sense beliefs, develop. On certain views of religion there will be overlap between the three, particularly if we take the religion to be grounded in or to involve what has happened to identifiable people in the past. But I am here interested less in overlap than in the independent growth of different webs. What has happened in the case of the Christian religion over the years may be described as web multiplication, which takes in not only the Christian religion, but other religions, and other areas of human culture. But here I am particularly interested in Christian belief and science or sciences.

Such webs, plural, are not restricted to religion—obviously not. Some of the time a person may conduct his thinking and action under strictly scientific auspices, seeking to understand matter in materialist ways and devising experiments accordingly. But he also may alongside this develop other sensitivities, to aesthetics or morals, say. The advantage of non-cognitivism in such a case is obvious, but suppose this person is a cognitivist in morals. Or maybe he is politically active, concerned with the immorality of the inequities in society. Then there is the problem of how the truths of morals (as he sees them) cohere with the truths of science. To do so, perhaps he divides himself as having a "private life" and a "public life."

Part of classical Christian thought is that God is one God, and that as a consequence, truth is one. That is, at least every truth is consistent with every other truth. Maybe such a religious person may travel some distance with non-cognitivism too. Besides, double truth has had its advocates, even among Christians, but not many. The idea that a proposition may be true-in-religion but not true-in-science has not caught on, for obvious reasons. But the growth of science on the one hand, and the structure of classical Christian thought on the other appear to have fractured the oneness of truth, or placed it in danger of fracture. For implicit in what I have argued in the first parts of this chapter is that the Christian faith is viable only if the sequence creation—fall—redemption is also viable.

It looks like that what we have here are at least two webs. This is an undesirable state of affairs for anyone, such as a Christian, who believes in the unity of truth. The important thing for a Christian is that natural science is provisional, revelation is not. Science is not simply an aggregation, but the ever-present activity of attempting to falsify present hypotheses. But the Christian faith is not revisable in the same way. It is carried forward in accordance with Christ's Great Commission. We know in part, due to our finitude and sin, and are continually in danger of falling into misunderstanding. For the Christian, his faith is not a falsifiable research project, which is not to say that the project is based on a "leap of faith" and not on relevant evidence.

To the Enlightenment mind this is unacceptable, since for such an outlook the earlier is the more primitive, while for the Christian the earlier has authority over the present. To make religion "relevant" to the current cultural outlook is not what is needed, though of course, like any decent communicator, the Christian ministry will look for points of contact with those outside the church.

This attitude, as far as it affects Christian anthropology, can be contrasted with, say, the practice of paleoanthropology, the success of which depends on the highly contingent incidence of ancient remains and on the success or failure of archaeological surveys for data, and perhaps the occurrence of singular events, such as the impact on the Earth of asteroids. Such data are contingent in their incidence and variable in their amount, and so it is not surprising that there few data may lead to a disproportionate revision in its hypotheses.

The state of paleoanthropology may be of considerable interest to Christians as well as to others, but the latest findings cannot be regarded as authoritative in any implications for original Christian anthropology. After all, the early anthropology of the Bible was the account of the Creation and then of the Fall, an account that is endorsed by Jesus and by the apostles. So, I suggest, the Christian's attitude in the face of such a state of affairs ought to be one of the suspense of his belief about the implications of empirically grounded beliefs for fundamental Christian doctrine. He should live in the hope that even in this life there will be a closer "fit" between the scientific account of early history and the biblical claims. After all, patience is a virtue.[7]

Such tension and perplexity that this engenders can be illustrated further from the attitude of the materialist philosopher to the data of consciousness and intentionality. In these data are evidence of a world of spirit. Can such data be given a materialist reduction or translation? It does not seem likely. There is a deep gulf—a difference in category—in the conceptuality of human intentionality and neuro-physical discharges and other goings-on in the brain. The prospect of identifying the one with the other seems remote, not a matter of the acquisition of more and more neuro-physical data, but of recognizing two different languages. There is no point in saying that the language of consciousness is "mythical." After all it is the basic language of humanity. And if it is mythical then what becomes of ethics, of good and evil? Indeed, what becomes of the entirety of human culture? This is not to make a point in science, but to suggest there is in science from time to time the same perplexity as in classical Christian theism, and the need for patience until, as a result of rethinking, the entire field becomes clearer. There is presumably a truth of the matter in which both physics and psychology figure. In terms of the possible relations between science and religion proposed by Ian Barbour, both this and the case of paleoanthropology are instances of what may be called "long-term integration" (1990, 23–37). Perhaps the Christian should think of such integration as an aspect of eschatology.

So there are real tensions here, no doubt, for the Christian, until time comes when we shall know even as we are known. Then, the Christian believes that the consistency of the findings of science will mesh with the fuller understanding of the revealed data. Until then Christians must live patiently, tolerating perplexity.

A final word

How do we treat the case of two sources of data each of which is well grounded but which conflict? What is our "belief-policy" to be in such a case?[8] This is a situation orthodox Christians are in. They have in consequence two webs of belief, one derived from their faith, and a web derived from science. I don't say that these are all the webs there are. There is the web of commonsense beliefs, which enables us to negotiate the everyday world of things and places, the immediate world of our five senses. But let us concentrate on these two worlds, those of science and faith.

It would be a mistake to characterize these webs as one of reason and one of faith. There are fideists, who characterize the distinction between reason (science) and that of faith (Christian orthodoxy) in terms of one between faith and reason. But this is in my view a mischaracterization. The world of science is one of reason, empirically informed reason beginning with the world of commonsense, and building on that via theoretic reason and the various devices that extend our senses, beginning with the telescope and the microscope, revealing (some say) the world as it really is as against the world of appearance. So a table is not solid, but consists of subatomic particles in rapid interaction. This physical theoretic world is one of generality and of provisionality. It is web-like with sets of propositions forming a hard core, with less and less well-entrenched propositions. A Popperian would emphasize falsifiability as the critical operation, either with law-like propositions or with their empirical derivations, or both, with the scientific community doing its best to falsify the empirical claim in question. The outer areas of the web are those of current dispute, debate, and perplexity among the scientific community. But the world of faith is not due to an irrational leap.

Once again, as an example let us consider the emergence of *homo sapiens*. The evidence-base of claims that *homo sapiens* first emerged in Africa, or Asia, or at multiple sites more or less simultaneously, is pretty thin, compared with, for example, some contemporary murder investigations. I imagine that a new set of discoveries in a new site would call the current theories of multiple sites into question. Perhaps given the present state of the data these multiple sites are the best that we can hope for. This is a natural human reaction. How firm should our present belief in multiple-site emergence be? However we answer that question it must recognize that current theories, or accounts, are provisional, but without current competitors, because there could be competitors and may be, so far unidentified.

Something like this, I suggest, obtains also in some of the sources in Christianity. It is important that this should be so. For the epochal events in Judeo-Christianity did not occur in La La Land but in the fresh air of the Middle East. Suppose that there was huge skepticism about whether there was a place named Galilee two thousand or so years ago. No Galilee, no Galilean. The point can be generalized. Of course, Christianity does not consist only in sets of facts of the Middle East. But such facts are necessary for Christianity to be what it claims to be, a way of salvation that depends on certain things occurring in certain times and places in accordance with their claims. More is needed than claims about the Middle East, but not less. But since it is a personally appropriable religion it has a personal side which behaves differently from the historical events, naturally. So here the "debate" is not simply a historical one, but encompasses the needs and hopes of men and women, boys and girls. The saving message of the Christian "gospel" either attracts or repels people. The narrative itself indicates this. That is, the overall narrative embraces not only straight history, but also an account of the reception, acceptance, and rejection, with a range of degrees of this. So, in an odd way, there is built in, in the words of its founder and his close associates, the conditions of mind that are to be found in those who receive it, and those who reject it.

Perhaps more should be said about this because it bears on the Christian's understanding of evil. Conventionally, there is a sharp distinction drawn in the "developed" West between what a person thinks and feels privately, and his public persona. And ethics, or virtue, has more of a public rather than a private character. This explains the sort of habits that are considered virtuous, for example, courage or temperance. It also explains the importance placed on utilitarianism in the history of ethics in the West, along with the centrality of questions of social justice. Christians should have regard to their neighbors, and there is a considerable overlap between the social ethics of Christians and of the secular world. But at the heart of Christianity is "the heart," that is the moral and spiritual center of the individual, which Jesus stresses. "Man looks on outward appearance, but the Lord looks on the heart" (1 Sam. 16:7). The stress falls on the purity of motive and the goodness of intention, the absence of hypocrisy and of double standards.

Here we touch upon the operation of divine grace in the lives of men and women, through which they are regenerated. It is reasonably referred to as a "new birth" or a "new creation" in the New Testament, which is the result of an operation on their inner selves, and in principle at least changes them, though they struggle with the effects of the "old man."

Notes

1 As one might expect, Plantinga provides a version which is consistent with his convictions regarding human indeterministic freedom and a Molinist approach to the counterfactuals of human freedom that ensues. Monism leads to God being the only source of evil, its permitter. However, a monism which is routed through incompatibilism and middle knowledge is different from a monism which is routed through compatibilism and sovereign grace.

2 Here, for the sake of economy, I shall omit reference to the interesting part that the devil plays in bringing about evil. But from the perspective of explanation, this is not more satisfying than stopping at human sin.

3 For Aquinas, for example, any creature is necessarily mutable (*ST* I Q 9, A 2, co.).

4 In such uses, "natural" connotes vestiges of the creation, not what is "usual" or "customary."

5 The idea of a web is due to W. V. O. Quine. See, for example, Quine and Ullian (1978).

6 For an application of the idea of a web to religious belief, see Helm (2000).

7 Here I am indebted to Hans Madeume (2014).

8 For more on the idea of a belief-policy, see Helm (1994).

Response to Paul Helm

Richard Brian Davis

Following Augustine, Paul Helm thinks of evil as a privation: "A deficiency or loss or negativity" (56). It "arises as a decline from the good" (ibid.). The explanation for how that could be in a world created by God is twofold. First, God ordains it; he permits (but doesn't cause) evil to occur. Secondly, since God is perfect, the moral evil he permits "can only arise from the creature" (55), that is, from human beings originally "created 'very good' by their Creator," but who "could change for the worse, and they did" (56).

Now these two sub-explanations, as Helm develops them, don't seem to me to fit together well. To see this, we must ask of the first: *why* does God permit evil? It is less than enlightening to reply, "It was the good pleasure of God that this is so" (55). For then the question arises: "Why is it the good pleasure of God that this is so?" (ibid.). Helm (following Plantinga) has an answer: the very best possible worlds contain incarnation and atonement and thus sin and evil. "For atonement is a matter of creatures' being saved from the consequences of their sin; therefore if there were no evil, there would be no sin" (Plantinga 2004, 12). So evil exists because God permits it, and he permits it because it's best. Without evil, there couldn't be the overriding good of incarnation and atonement.

It isn't necessary to descend into the details here.[1] My point is simply that this sub-explanation is incompatible with the second: that evil arises by way of human agency and choice. For there aren't any of these incarnation and atonement worlds for God to choose from, if in fact evil cannot arise. And given Helm's Calvinistic commitments, it can't. Let me explain.

On Helm's view, all of the evil in the world is ultimately traceable to "the Fall"—a free and deliberate choice to disobey God by the original human pair he created. As the story goes, they were commanded not to eat the fruit, and warned that it would be fatal if they did. Alas, they decided to eat it. Call this choice DISOBEY—the first evil. It "is not clear" says Helm (57), how DISOBEY could transpire if (as he thinks) everything God created was "very good." Indeed, he says it is a "mystery." But of course a confession of "necessary ignorance" (ibid.) isn't anything like an *explanation* for evil. Helm is sure of one thing, however—that choice was determined:

> It is important to stress that such a choice was not a libertarian choice. The original position was not one of neutrality, but that in which human beings were created "very good" by their Creator. It was not that the way of life [not eating the fruit] and the way of death [eating the fruit] were equidistant or otherwise symmetrically before the chooser. (56)

Having said this, Helm promptly invokes *compatibilism*: that "human action is both determined and [yet] . . . the agent is responsible for what he does or fails to do" (57). So Helm wants us to see that the choice is determined. But then if it's the agent who is responsible for DISOBEY, why not say *he* caused the act? Helm doesn't give us much to go on here, but he does point us to Jonathan Edwards (ibid.).[2]

According to Edwards, if a volition (like DISOBEY) lacks a motive, a reason for acting, it has no end or aim and thus fails to "exert any inclination" toward anything. But this is incoherent, says Edwards, since a choice necessarily involves the will moving "by an act of preference and inclination" (1754 [1957], 225). This entitles us to infer

> MOTIVE: "Every act of the will (volition) is excited by a motive" (ibid.).

Now MOTIVE is ambiguous. It can be read as expressing a kind of ground-consequent relation obtaining between motives and volitions, in which case it tells us that

> MOTIVE$_1$: Every act of the will (volition) is occasioned by a motive.

That is to say, a volition is *informed by* its motive—that motive being the ground, basis, or reason for which one decides to act. But if motives are reasons for acting, they are at best abstract considerations. It's simply a category mistake to think they are causes. The agent retains the power to act on a given motive or to refrain. I see nothing at all objectionable in reading MOTIVE this way. It happily leaves room for DISOBEY to count as an original sin or first evil for which Helm's original humans could be held accountable.

But that's not how Edwards (and I suspect Helm) sees the matter. On the Helm-Edwards reading, we should interpret MOTIVE as expressing a Cause-Effect relation. That is, we should read it as

MOTIVE$_2$: Every act of the will (volition) is caused by a motive.

Thus, volitions are said to be effects "necessarily connected with their motives," which operate "by biassing the will, and giving it a certain inclination or preponderation one way" (Edwards [1754] 1957, 225–26). Now if that's right, the original (non-neutral, non-indifferent) position in which Helm's humans were created involved God's giving their wills "a certain inclination" toward "the way of life." He did this no doubt by giving them the relevant (causally necessitating) motive, say,

M1: Refraining from eating that fruit will satisfy my desire to obey God and prevent my own death ["the way of life"].

But here we strike a problem. For if MOTIVE$_2$ is true, and if God causally necessitates that those original humans have M1, it will be causally impossible that DISOBEY ever occur and hence that evil ever arise. (This conclusion generalizes across worlds.)

Consequently, if evil really does result from "the chooser" moving "away from the original position" (56), there must be a *stronger* motive, stronger even than the God-instilled motive M1, if that were possible. What could that motive be? If we're following Helm's biblical account (and I'm not averse), it is roughly this:

M2: Eating that fruit will satisfy my desire for food and for gaining wisdom ["the way of death"].

Now these two motivations, M1 and M2, run at cross-purposes. The conjunction of M2 and MOTIVE$_2$ causally necessitates DISOBEY.

The conjunction of M1 and MOTIVE$_2$ causally precludes it. Helm must now face a dilemma. Either those original humans chose to act on M2 rather than M1 or they didn't. If they did, then (by MOTIVE$_2$) there was a third motive that caused *that* choice. You can see where this goes. We're looking at an infinite regress of motives for choosing between motives. Whence, then, DISOBEY?

If, on the other hand, those original humans didn't choose M2 over M1, but instead were directly caused to act on M2, we can rightly ask what that cause was. By hypothesis, everything was created "very good." Therefore, nothing in their nature or circumstances can be to blame. Assuming that M2 isn't uncaused, that leaves either God Himself or that original human pair *qua* agent-causes. Helm and Edwards sadly reject the latter option. Where does that leave them? In a theological fix, I submit. Indeed, Helm is ultimately driven to admit:

> It is difficult for some to see how compatibilism can be so without God being the author of sin. Or how under compatibilist auspices evil can be culpable. This is certainly a problem. (57)

It certainly is . . . for the theological determinist. And if this is the way things go across worlds, then sin and evil won't so much as present themselves as possibilities. Tragically then, there won't be incarnation and atonement worlds for God to actualize. This is because there won't be any worlds in which we human beings fall into sin, and in which an incarnate God can redeem us from our evil. Knowing my own moral shortcomings, I don't want to live in a modal universe like that. Happily, for the agent-causal theist cleaving to MOTIVE$_1$, there is no such transworld moral abyss to face.

Michael Ruse

With Paul Helm, we are in the world of John Calvin, not Charles Darwin. I shall take the discussion from there and I focus on the problem that Helm poses, namely why a good God, who is totally sovereign, would allow evil in His creation. It is, as Helm notes, not a problem for a nonbeliever like me, although I suspect he and I would differ on whether I can truly have evil in my world, or if it is not really all a question of nasty things happening to people, whether thanks to Himmler or thanks to smallpox.

I see two important moves in Helm's Calvinist world. First, sin is a function of free will. As a Calvinist, of course, Helm believes in a compatibilist form of free will. So do I, so we are not going to quarrel there. The point is that we do have a meaningful sense of free will, and (for Helm) it was better that God make people free to sin, rather than make them automata who would never do anything wrong. Better a world with a free Himmler, with all of the awful consequences, than a world of robots, with no such consequences. God is free, we are made in His image, and free will is part of the package deal. But why should we sin? Why aren't we just good all of the time, like God Himself? Because of original sin. Adam ate the fruit, and that was it. The Fall. Adam was tainted and that taint gets passed on to us all. (How the taint works need not concern us here. Catholics think something is laid on our good God-given nature. Protestants think that our good God-given nature is corrupted, in a sense.)

The second move is God fixing the sin. This is where the crucifixion comes in. Jesus is a blood sacrifice atoning for our sin. The key passage is from Paul's Epistle to the Romans. "For as by one man's disobedience [Adam] many were made sinners, so by the obedience of one [Jesus] shall many be made righteous" (Rom. 5:19). Jesus is the Lamb of God. He had to be the son of God however, for no lesser a sacrifice would do. You could hang up as many philosophy grad students as you like and it still wouldn't do the trick. Now all of this sounds pretty awful, and makes the whole drama seem like Plan B. Humans let the side down—Adam did, at least—and so God had to scramble, to improvise, to fix it. Not a bit of it, argues Helm. The need for an act of crucifixion was a lucky accident. *O Felix Culpa!* By the sacrifice, we had such an act of love that it topped everything that had happened, canceled out all of the bad things, and so we are ahead of a world in which Adam did what he was told, we are all good, and Jesus could stay home.

This is not a stupid answer. I always say that Saint Augustine and Saint Anselm and Saint Thomas and the others make me truly proud to be a philosopher. If you look at my response to Richard Brian Davis, you can properly infer that I include Jonathan Edwards in my list, and not at the bottom. These are mega-minds. However, it is a horrifically wrong answer. For a start, the whole idea of substitutionary atonement is ethically repellent. That someone should die screaming in agony for my sins is morally repulsive and the same applies to a Being who demands this for satisfaction. It is a dreadful relict of past pagan practices and I want no part of it.

For a second, I am a free being and what an ancestor did many years ago is neither here nor there. Of course, parents can ruin a child's life—fetal alcohol syndrome is a start and systematic sexual abuse is a second—but my parents were not like that and I doubt yours were either. In turn, my wife and I have been very loving parents. We did not do everything right but to say that our kids are tainted by our sins is just nonsense. For a third, Adam and Eve did not exist (Ruse 2012a). Probably human evolution did involve bottlenecks but never less than about ten thousand, and while we may all have descended from at least one of this group, we are also as likely to have all descended from many in the group. Moreover, there was no point at which sin suddenly appeared. Our mums and dads going way back were just like us—sometimes good, sometimes bad, a bit of a mix.

I know there are gambits that are played to save original sin in the face of the truths of human evolution. Reinhold Niebuhr (1941, 1943) talked of Adam and Eve as being symbolic. But symbolic of what? A cigar is a symbol of a penis. What is the penis in this particular case? In any case, as Freud said, sometimes a good cigar is just a smoke. Why are Adam and Eve not just a good smoke? You might say that evolution comes to the rescue. I thought this once. "Original sin is part of the biological package. It comes with being human. We inherit it from our parents and they from their parents: they acted as they did, and because they acted as they did, it is passed down to us" (Ruse 2001, 210). It just won't do. God created us good. Our original nature could not be bettered. That is why the death on the cross has nothing to do with this essential part of human nature. Ten deaths on the cross would have no effect on our regular appetites or need of sleep. The death on the cross speaks to the changes wrought by sin. If our animal nature—our ferocity and nastiness—is now part of our biology, the death can have no more effect than on the need of eating and drinking and sleeping. It is created by God and hence in some sense has to be considered good.

As far as *felix culpa* is concerned, the less said the better. It is grotesquely insensitive to say that the death of Anne Frank in Bergen-Belsen or of Sophie Scholl of the White Rose group under the guillotine is canceled by even a thousand crucifixions. Apart from anything else, you don't have to be an ardent Kantian to see that you are using these deaths as a means to an end—the glory of the crucifixion. That is immoral. Augustine saw this, of course (Ruse 2018). In fighting a war, you cannot just go out and slaughter innocents to achieve your ends. And everything has to be proportional. That is why so many like Elizabeth Anscombe (1957) spoke against Truman and the Bomb. The destruction could never justify the ends. Any system which allows the Holocaust is morally rotten.

I sound as though I, an admitted nonbeliever, am being very anti-Christian. This is not so. I am being very anti-Calvinist. There is another tradition which I, brought up as a Quaker, find far more empathetic—incarnational theology. This is a theology based on the Jesus of the Gospels, not Paul of the Epistles. Here Jesus is seen as a friend who came to give us a model. Nietzsche, of all people, expressed it best. "This 'bringer of glad tidings' died as he lived, as he *taught*—*not* to redeem mankind, but to demonstrate how one ought to live" (1895, 159). He died on the cross as an example of true love, for us to follow. There was no apple eating. There was no Fall. There was no expulsion. Serpents are off the hook. There is therefore no need for the bloody sacrifice on the cross. The Son of God is the loving friend—the Jesus we see with Martha and Mary in Vermeer's great painting—rather than the tortured wretch on the cross—the Jesus of Grünewald. There is evil, due to human free will. We are responsible, not God. He loves us for all of our weaknesses and comes to help and guide and encourage. That, to be honest, is a God worth worshiping, not the God of the Calvinist.

I do not believe in the existence of God. Out of deep gratitude, I have spent the whole of my life trying to follow His example.

Erik J. Wielenberg

In his exposition of "compatibilistic Christianity," Helm tackles the theological problem of evil, appealing to Plantinga's "*felix culpa*" theodicy to explain the presence of evil in the world. The *felix culpa* theodicy is a central element of Helm's view, and in this reply I develop some doubts about its adequacy. Specifically, I question (a) whether divine atonement for sin has the sort of value that the *felix culpa* theodicy seems to require and (b) whether the presence of psychopaths in the world is compatible with the *felix culpa* theodicy and Helm's compatibilist Christianity. I offer these challenges not as decisive refutations of Helm's view but rather as invitations to him to say more.

A central element of Helm's approach to the theological problem of evil is the "God-centeredness" (52) of the universe. This is the idea that God's ultimate goal in creating the universe is to display His power and goodness; as Helm puts it, "The universe is arranged for God's good pleasure, or for the display of his perfection" (ibid.). God is perfect whether or not He creates a universe; His ultimate goal in creating a universe is to *display* the perfection of His divine nature. Drawing on Plantinga's development of the *felix culpa* theodicy, Helm suggests that God's incarnation and atonement for the sins of humanity are essential elements of the display of divine perfection. Since there can be no atonement without sin to be atoned for, and sin produces a lot of (further) evil, God's display of His perfection requires the presence of sin and evil in the world.

Helm appears to lump together divine incarnation and atonement and view their conjunction as the great good that justifies the presence of sin in the world. He says that "a world including the incarnation of the Son of God is immeasurably better than one without it, since the incarnation involves the humbling of the eternal God for our sakes and for our salvation" (54). However, as Kevin Diller (2008, 91), Marilyn Adams (2008), and Michael Peterson (2012, 184–85) all point out, God's incarnation in human form and God's atonement for the sins of humanity are logically distinct and it seems possible for the former to occur without the latter. Since divine incarnation does not require the presence of sin or evil in the world, if the *felix culpa* theodicy is to work there must be tremendous value specifically in divine atonement for human sin. I am skeptical that there is enough value in divine atonement to outweigh the evil of the sin that is atoned for. Consider these two claims:

(i) Given the existence of sin, it is better that the sin is atoned for than that it remains unatoned for.

(ii) The atonement of sin is so good that it is better that there be atoned-for sin than that there be no sin in the first place.

Claim (i) seems plausible; however, the *felix culpa* theodicy seems to require something like claim (ii) rather than claim (i), and (ii) does not seem plausible. The point of atonement is to make up for or set right sin that has occurred. As Eleonore Stump explains, the essence of atonement is the setting right of the "absence of unity between God and human beings" (2012, 129). Accordingly, it seems that atonement can at best cancel the evil of sin, returning the overall balance of good and evil to zero; I don't see a plausible basis for holding that atonement—as distinguished from divine incarnation—could make the overall combination of sin and atonement into a good.

Diller considers the thought that "there is a special excellence to the quality of relationship that can be known by those once lost who are redeemed" (2008, 93). The thought here is that (ii) is true in virtue of the great value in the relationship between God and humans who have been alienated and then reconciled with God. However, as Diller points out, it is hard to see how to justify (ii) on such grounds without thereby committing oneself to such implausible claims as "the strongest marriages are those that have involved a period of divorce, or that the deepest mother-daughter relationship is enabled once the daughter commits patricide" (2008, 93). Furthermore, such grounds for (ii) suggest that greater degrees of alienation make possible more valuable goods of reconciliation later on. In the case of sin, that line of thinking appears to lead to the following problem: "If sin is the occasioning cause of grace . . . then shouldn't the upright man try to overcome his repugnance to sin, and commit still *more* sins?" (Scarre 2009, 22). Acceptance of (ii) and the *felix culpa* theodicy suggests that more sin enhances the overall value of the world, all things considered—a dubious implication.

A final challenge for (ii) is presented by Michael Peterson, who argues that (ii) is incompatible with "the classical Christian doctrine of creation" (2012, 184). Peterson writes,

> God's original purpose is to invite finite personal creatures into an intimate relationship with himself. Indeed, the historic Christian vision of the human *telos* is that we are meant for participation in the divine Trinitarian life. This entails that God works faithfully to bring our *telos* to fulfillment, such that the highest good for creation is available without creation's descent into sin and evil. (2012, 184–85)

While I can hardly claim to have shown that (ii) is false, it seems to have some unwelcome implications. Accordingly, I invite Helm to provide some support for (ii) and to respond to the worries I've raised.

A second challenge for the *felix culpa* theodicy arises from the presence in our world of what Adams calls "wrecked and ruined human agency" (2008, 134). Her examples of such agency include the following: "Agency that is hardened and biochemically twisted (serial killers, child sex murderers, schizophrenics), agency that is biologically or psychologically too fragmented . . . to be capable of whole-hearted commitment to anything" (2008, 134). Adams's worry is that God would be insufficiently loving and merciful toward such wrecked and ruined human agents were He to create them in order to display His perfection through divine atonement (see also Diller 2008, 93–95).

One important type of deficient agency not explicitly mentioned by Adams is psychopathy. Psychopaths are incapable of empathy, love, or guilt and cannot grasp the authority of moral demands. As Robert Hare, a psychologist who has studied psychopaths for over a quarter of a century explains, psychopaths lack "the shackles of a nagging conscience" (1993, 75–76; see also Stout 2005 and Kiehl 2014). Psychologist Cordelia Fine and philosopher Jeanette Kennett say that for psychopaths, "moral . . . rules are annoying restrictions to be manipulated or ignored. None of these rules have normative force for them" (2008, 175). Psychopaths lack the emotional capacity to grasp the weight of morality and, because they are devoid of guilt, see no need for any of their actions to be atoned for. It is hard to see why the existence of this particular sort of damaged agency is necessary for the great good of divine atonement. God could have omitted psychopaths from His grand plan without sacrificing the need for atonement. Indeed, Helm appears to claim that God did omit psychopaths from His grand plan. Helm says that through the Fall human beings lost their "knowledge of God and the personal holiness and righteousness that went with it" but retain a "moral sense that has outlasted . . . the Fall" (58). He further declares that "human beings, unlike sheep, have a conscience, a moral sense which they can apply to themselves and others. So things are not as bad as they could be" (ibid.). However, there is ample evidence from psychology to suggest that things *are* as bad as they could be—at least for a minority of human beings, psychopaths who lack a moral sense altogether. Hare puts it this way:

> The psychopath is like a color-blind person who sees the world in shades of gray but who has learned how to function in a colored world. He has learned that the light signal for "stop" is at the top of the traffic light. When the color-blind person tells you he stopped at the *red* light, he really means he stopped at the *top* light. . . . Like the color-blind person, the psychopath lacks an important element of experience—in this case, emotional experience—but may have learned the words that others use to describe or mimic experiences that he cannot really understand. (1993, 129)

The existence of the wrecked and ruined agency of psychopaths seems mysterious both in the context of Helm's Christian compatibilism and the *felix culpa* theodicy. Again, I do not claim to have shown that there is no way that the presence of psychopaths in the world can be reconciled with Helm's overall picture of things, but on the face of it there seems to be a mismatch here. In sum, then, I offer these remarks as encouragement to Helm to say something in defense of principle (ii) above—the claim that the atonement of sin is so good that it is better that there be atoned-for sin than that there be no sin in the first place—as well as about how psychopaths fit into his view of things.

Notes

1 For details, see Davis and Franks (2018).

2 Here I leave aside Helm's Edwardsian strawman, namely, that if DISOBEY were self-determined, then prior to that *first* sinful volition (i.e., DISOBEY) there was another sinful volition the choice to disobey. But this reasoning is confused. To say that a decision is self-determined doesn't mean that it results from the agent's choosing to decide. Rather, as the term suggests, if it is *self*-determined, it is the agent *herself* who stands as the first, uncaused cause of the decision.

Reply to Critics

Paul Helm

I thank my three colleagues for their kind attention to my chapter. My general outlook is that a Christian philosopher is to be what John Locke referred to as "an underlabourer in clearing ground a little" (1689, 10), the more so considering that our moral and spiritual plight involves mysterious things and states.

The attitude of contemporary philosophy and science is that philosophy can or should explain evil, or science can or should. Modernity is the permanent normal, because we now inhabit what Hume called "these enlightened ages." Or if the explanation does not follow enlightenment parameters, then there is no such evil or it's not what we thought it was. I say that what Christians have traditionally held is that *history* can or should locate the explanation, and then only by making assumptions that we don't like, or are not fashionable. The Christian faith can be represented as a web of belief with a central focus and interrelated threads. Both the central focus is mysterious, as are some of the outliers. The Christian pilgrim-church lies somewhere in the intermediate network of threads. My comments on the arguments of my fellow contributors come from this set of assumptions.

Michael Ruse

Ruse nicely illustrates my point. He notes that the world of Calvin is different from that of Darwin. Generalizing, the world of classical Christianity is different from that of the Enlightenment. But Ruse also, interestingly, distinguishes between natural selection as a scientific hypothesis, or a set of such, and natural selection as a religion, an Explanation of Everything. The latter of which he

eschews. It's a valid distinction. A classical Christian understands
and accepts the mechanisms of natural selection, but does not offer
it as the Grand Explanation of everything, easily finely tunable
by nonchalantly adding or subtracting millions of years or by
introducing the effect of the odd large meteorite in the story—were
it that easy.

There is also the particular issue of how processes of natural
selection alone lead to the development of intentionality, of the
"aboutness" of consciousness. This gap is an embarrassment
to naturalist philosophers. Ruse says nothing about it. But as a
naturalist he is driven, it seems, to confess his ignorance of those
mechanisms at work in the alleged shift from preconscious to fully
conscious states, for there seems to be no natural step which counts
as becoming human from prehuman parents. Natural selection may
be a blind watchmaker, but it is inconceivable as a blind soul-maker.
Is this not a gaping lacuna in explanation? Why silence?

It seems that Ruse thinks of what I wrote as including the free
will defense. He and I are each compatibilists. It would be better
for me to think of sin as a function of mutable human nature and
of divine permission. But we must leave this in order to discuss his
detection of "God's fixing of sin" in the crucifixion of Jesus. Which
is not, in his view, a "stupid answer" (70). Nonetheless he thinks
the crucifixion was repellent, which is an interesting response of
someone who is an ethical skeptic, or of one who aspires to be
one. This is far from the claim that sin was "fixed" by the one who
agonized on the cross, who was there by his choice and his Father's
will, a choice motivated by selfless love.

In contrast to the traditional, biblical Christian position, of
redemption through the blood of the Cross, Ruse makes his own
position clear. He favors an incarnation-based, exemplarist view.
And indeed, it is tempting to sanitize things. Being made sin is horror.
Ruse endorses the individualism of the West which has no place for
either the curse of sin or the blessings of the imputation of Christ's
righteousness. The race was cursed in the fall of Adam, and Christ
endured that for our sakes. Ruse is further evidence that modern
people have no time for the idea of a curse—except in fiction—as
something comic, associated with witches and broomsticks. How
else to explain universal lawlessness? Philosophers also have no
time for it in their ethical reflections, but our plight is misunderstood
if we do not take it seriously. We are under the curse, and Christ

became a curse for us. That is, he lifted our curse. All these matters are not so much directly pertinent to the explanation of evil, which is our joint project, as to its alleviation.

It is in the last phase of his rejoinder that Ruse offers his sanitized version of Christianity. He writes of the taint of evil (70), and of his preference for an incarnational theology because of its moral higher tone, rid of the shedding of blood which is so central to New Testament soteriology (72), and with no need to rely upon the particularities of history. In such sanitized theology, the *idea* of such a Jesus-figure would suffice equally well. The idea of Jesus as an inspirational example and no more. But as we shall note in the comments on Wielenberg's similar move this, though popular, strays beyond the parameters of the New Testament.

Richard Davis

Davis thinks my case is spoiled by advancing two inconsistent claims (66). In my lead essay I claimed that arguments of this type, that God could not do certain things without permitted conditions, were of a general character, and that the *felix culpa* argument is one such. Davis thinks that this is at odds with the idea that evil arises by way of human agency and free choice (66) and he goes on to explain this. This dislocation is because everything God created was very good. And that is not an explanation, simply a confession of ignorance. Why not say that the agent caused the act because she is responsible for what she does or fails to do.

Philosophy takes us only so far in understanding unique factual situations. I do not admit the difficulty reluctantly, for this is where philosophy cannot help in the case of the intersection of divine and human action. Agent-causation—*in se* another mysterious matter, it seems to me—fares no better.

Davis himself goes astray here. I do not say that there is no (human) cause for what transpired, but that it is hard to see what that cause was. Maybe naiveté, or self-deception, or an overweening will, as Descartes once suggested. I see the problem. It is irritating to a philosopher to have to recognize such a gap in our understanding. But I guess that an indeterminist has the gap too. How can there be a rebellious free choice from an individual who has been created "very good"?

The answer has been that "very good" is an initial state of sinlessness, but possessed by one whose state is "mutable." This has to be distinguished from the state of being "as good as can be," the state of immutable sinlessness, that enjoyed through grace by the redeemed in heaven. The lapse into sin is possible because of mutability; it provided a window of opportunity. This provides the possibility of an explanation of rebellion. But as we are not familiar with the psychology of human mutable sinlessness, of what can motivate the slide into sin, we are left with analogies and metaphors.

Davis complains that my two sub-explanations don't seem to fit together (66). Why did God permit evil? The regress of explanation has to stop somewhere. If we aren't party to the reasons, or they are given but unintelligible, then—mystery. For his part, Davis invokes his agent-causal theory of human freedom. But I do not see how this fares any better. His view of freedom as the indeterminate power of agent-causation is that it is not a function of the faculty of the will, say, but of the total self, the agent. To say that a decision is self-determined doesn't mean that it results from the agent's choosing to decide. Rather, as the term suggests, "It is *self*-determined, it is the agent *herself* who stands as the first, uncaused cause of the decision" (76fn2; emphasis in original). Invoking a creaturely unmoved mover does not seem an advance. For human freedom is usually regarded as an event, or a series of such. Assuming the self is a substance, how does it change from one state, a substance choosing A, to another, a substance choosing B? How is that substantial change to be understood?

I think that the reason for Davis's criticism involving senses of "motive" is the idea that if motives are causes this must mean that God causes evil actions. That is, it boils down to the old "author of sin" objection. But the language of that objection is vague, ambiguous. That phrase "the author of sin" cries out for further analysis, something that Davis is well able to undertake. Why then does he not do so? Here perhaps motives are also relevant. Incidentally, I am not "driven" to an admission of the force of the objection, as he opines (69), but in fact I reject its force. What I said was not that this presents an insurmountable difficulty, but that it is difficult for some to see how it can be so without God being the author of sin. But for some time I have not regarded this as the problem it is reckoned to be.[1] I wonder that Davis, with his acute sense of argument, does not spot the fact that the phrase "the author of sin," predicated of such an infinite, immaculate Spirit as God is, is metaphorical. As Guillaume Bignon says, in his excellent discussion, "God is not a human being, holding a pen and writing a book" (2018, 180). And being that, the rational course is to see in what *sense* God is the author of sin when he ordains or permits states of affairs that an infinite, holy spirit could be responsible for, and what not.

Erik J. Wielenberg

Wielenberg has kindly invited me to say more (73). This requires me to discuss the relation between the incarnation and the atonement. And in the few words remaining I would like to try to oblige. Taking up my *felix culpa* approach Wielenberg wonders whether divine atonement for sin has the sort of value that the *felix culpa* theodicy seems to require. And later on, he wonders whether the presence in the world of psychopaths is consistent with that theodicy and with my compatibilist Christianity. What he objects to is that in that theodicy, divine incarnation and atonement are lumped together. They are indeed separable ideas, and he cites a number of contemporary thinkers who trade on this to offer that there are possible worlds in which there is, for example, incarnation without sin and thus without the need of atonement. The background of these various ideas is the root idea of the "incarnation anyway" speculation, the idea that given the creation, it was inevitable that God would display his glory by becoming incarnate. To which I reply that the consistent attitude is not to speculate, but instead take full account of the scriptural account in which the two are tied together. To speculate on different outcomes from those in which incarnation and atonement in fact go together may show ingenuity and imagination, but not Christian consistency. Wielenberg thinks that incarnation is not worth the trouble if God's glory could be displayed without it. The price of the course he recommends is to treat "atonement" as an abstract idea, as in his suggestions about sin and atonement, which goes directly against the tenor of the New Testament.

One of these abstractions that he cites, that of Diller, that the upright man should try to overcome his repugnance to sin and commit more sin to enhance the divine atonement (74) came up in the early years of Christianity. The Apostle Paul (Rom. 6.15) asks the rhetorical question, that (if we are saved by grace) should we not go on sinning that grace may abound? Being fully Trinitarian, divine atonement in the New Testament is a conceptually complex business. It has to do not only with a "payment" but one such as would also secure the renovation of human character, in which (the *felix culpa* theodicist would add) God is further glorified. The philosopher's appetite for hard cases and thought experiments ought not to blur the barriers between one concept and another.

Similar abstractionism occurs in Peterson as reported by Wielenberg (74):

> God's original purpose is to invite finite personal creatures into an intimate personal relationship with himself. Indeed, the historic Christian vision of the human *telos* is that we are meant for participation in the divine Trinitarian life. This entails that God works faithfully to bring our *telos* to fulfillment, such that the highest good for creation without creation's descent into sin and evil. (2012, 184–85)

Though some of this proposal is not altogether clear, what is clear is that Peterson's proposal is far from the New Testament.

Wielenberg's second challenge (75) has to do the *felix culpa*'s failure to reach examples of what the late Marilyn Adams called "wrecked and ruined human agency" (2008, 134). Interrogating the New Testament about a list of such hard cases also has a long history. What about the variously incapacitated children who die in infancy, and those people who have not as much as heard whether there is an individual named Jesus Christ? Wielenberg's psychopaths join this list. The New Testament does not address these directly, but its offer of an eschatology in which many that are first will be last and the last first (Mt. 19:30), seems to provide plenty of scope for the restoration and redemption of such.

Note

1 See Helm (1988, 160) and more recently in Helm (2010). See also, Bignon (2018, Part II).

3

Evil and Atheistic
Moral Skepticism

Michael Ruse

Let me start with the most important statement in this essay. I believe in the existence of evil. I think some people are truly evil human beings. Heinrich Himmler for one. Let me add a couple more important things. I don't think everyone is evil all of the time—"total depravity," to use the Calvinist term. That sort of thing. "The God that holds you over the pit of hell, much as one holds a spider or some loathsome insect over the fire, abhors you, and is dreadfully provoked. His wrath towards you burns like fire; he looks upon you as worthy of nothing else but to be cast into the fire" (Edwards 1741, 411). This strikes me as both false and morally unhealthy. Sophie Scholl of the Munich White Rose group, who went to the guillotine for opposing Hitler, leaves me humbled by her transcendent goodness. This said, all of us do things that are wrong—are jealous, covet, bend the truth to our ends, and much more. There are levels of wrongdoing. Being rude to your mum is wrong, but hardly evil on the level of, let us say, the Catholic priests and young children.

So I believe in evil; for all that I am a moral skeptic or non-realist or some such thing. I am with my hero David Hume. I don't see philosophical skepticism as denying the existence of what you are talking about—causality, free will, moral truths, evil. Evil exists and, by "evil," I mean something with a value component. Heinrich Himmler was someone with bad values; Sophie Scholl was someone with good values. However, I do see my skepticism as something trying to give an analysis that does not depend on God or Platonic forms or whatever. My philosophy begins and ends with what it is to be a human being, to know and work with the world of experience. I think this is the philosophy of David Hume; certainly in his spirit. That I am a Humean and not something new makes me comfortable. My experience is that when someone says they have something entirely new, it is usually either stupid or (as Whitehead would insist) to be found in Plato. Although I defer to no one in my admiration for Plato—he makes me proud to be a philosopher— I don't particularly want to be stuck with either of those disjuncts. To borrow from the hymn—"If it's good enough for David Hume, then it's good enough for me."

Natural evil

Begin the discussion with one of the simple truths that you learn in Philosophy 101. When dealing with the problem of evil, it is customary to divide the topic into two—natural evil, earthquakes and the like, and moral evil, packing Jews off to Auschwitz and the like. There are major differences between the two, but they are brought under the same term "evil," because they both involve things that humans do not want or much like. You would rather not be crushed by a falling building brought on by a shifting of the continental plates. You don't want to be set upon by robbers. You don't want to boil to death rather unpleasantly in the overheated desert. Although showing that you cannot draw an entirely strict line between natural and moral evil, the overheating could well be a function both of the peculiarities of the terrain as well as of global warming, which brings in human action. This is what moral evil is all about. Himmler did not have to give orders leading to the extermination of the Jews. He had a choice and he chose to kill. Note that goodness is the reverse of this. A falling stone is not morally evil if it simply slipped and fell. It is morally evil if I set out deliberately to drop it on your head.

To clear the ground, let me say first a few things about natural evil and then I can turn to moral evil. I am a philosophical skeptic, which I suppose in a sense means that I don't accept God—I am an atheist or at least an agnostic.[1] In approaching something like earthquakes I have already, at least implicitly, ruled out putting them in a theological context. I am just not talking about whether God makes them happen because he is mad at us—Old Testament Yahweh behavior—or because he is testing us—New Testament Jesus behavior. I want to make it clear that although (as I shall show) I do think that evil impinges on the God question, I am not a nonbeliever because of—certainly not primarily because of—the problem of evil. I am a nonbeliever because I cannot get away from the nasty suspicion that it is all made up. I will speak of Christianity in this essay, although I would be prepared to extend my skepticism across the board, beginning with the Mormons. I think Christianity is a powerful and sophisticated religion, but I think it was constructed by believers in the early centuries after Christ—prominently beginning with Paul and as prominently ending with Augustine. In particular, theologically Christianity is a clever but ultimately unsuccessful fusion of Greek philosophy and Jewish theology. This leads to a fundamental paradox at the heart of the religion, about the nature of God. On the one hand, God in Platonic fashion is taken to be eternal, unchanging, outside time and space. This means that, although we can supposedly know of him through analogy, he has some very nonhuman features. Anselm draws this line of thinking to its conclusion: "For when thou beholdest us in our wretchedness, we experience the effect of compassion, but thou dost not experience the feeling" (Anselm 1903, 13). Likewise Aquinas: "To sorrow, therefore, over the misery of others does not belong to God" (*ST* I, Q 21, A 3, co.). Yet, on the other hand, the Jewish God is a person. He made a covenant with Abraham. For all that he has to punish him, he loves David as someone rather special—as do we all. He is the father in the parable of the prodigal son. It is he who Jesus on the Cross feels has forsaken him and yet also he to whom Jesus turns in the end. "Father, into thy hands I commend my spirit" (Lk. 23:46). These are two different notions and they don't mix. Oil and water. Nice try but no cigar.

For a nonbeliever like me therefore the problem of natural evil is a nonproblem. For all of my earlier declarations, I don't believe in it! Of course, I believe that there are all sorts of unpleasant things that happen to us and to the rest of the organic world: falling rocks, out-of-control fires, predators, diseases. I don't think of them as being evil, in the sense of things that have a value component. They just are. Although I do not share his fervent hatred of religion, I am with Richard Dawkins on this.

> In a universe of blind physical forces and genetic replication, some people are going to get hurt, other people are going to get lucky, and you won't find any rhyme or reason in it, nor any justice. The universe we observe has precisely the properties we should expect if there is, at bottom, no design, no purpose, no evil and no good, nothing but blind, pitiless indifference. (Dawkins 1995, 133)

Of course, it is still open to ask even a nonbeliever like me why it is that there is so much natural evil around—if we may continue to use the term "evil," however interpreted (Ruse 2001). Open to ask me, although I am not sure I am obliged to respond. I don't know why the world is as it is. It just is. Of course, we can say a bit more. If we are going to have a functioning world, a world in which humans can and do live, then some rules and restrictions have to apply. We cannot sit on hot stoves and expect nothing to happen. Either we have to give up on cooking—a diet of raw carrots forever and a day?—or we have got to have some kind of warning device. I suppose that logically it is possible that we might have evolved with neon lights in the middle of our foreheads that flash when we are in danger of burning, but a short sharp pain is surely as effective and a lot cheaper to produce in biological terms. Whether or not you want to treat the pains from burns as evil or not, one can see good reasons why they are around, even if sometimes they are extreme and even counterproductive.

One can go a bit further than this. Charles Darwin worried a lot about the pain and suffering caused by his mechanism of evolution through natural selection. Shortly after the *Origin of Species* was published in 1859, he wrote to his good friend the American botanist Asa Gray:

> With respect to the theological view of the question; this is always painful to me.—I am bewildered.—I had no intention to write atheistically. But I own that I cannot see, as plainly as others do, & as I sh^d. wish to do, evidence of design & beneficence on all sides of us. There seems to me too much misery in the world.

I cannot persuade myself that a beneficent & omnipotent God would have designedly created the Ichneumonidae with the express intention of their feeding within the living bodies of caterpillars, or that a cat should play with mice. Not believing this, I see no necessity in the belief that the eye was expressly designed. (Darwin [1860] 1993, 224)

Well, if you are a nonbeliever like me, then none of this is a problem—at least, not philosophically or theologically. Pain and suffering happens. Get over it. This said, you might wonder if we need quite all of the pain and suffering. It is almost as if we have an argument for an evil God. Such misery has to have a reason. Actually, I agree on this, but I don't think it leads you to or from God. Dawkins (1983) of all people offers a solution. He argues that the only way we can get the evolution of functioning organisms—adaptations like the hand and the eye—is through an unguided, rather brutal mechanism like selection. All of the alternatives, like Lamarckism—the inheritance of acquired characteristics—don't work empirically and are philosophically flawed, because they rely on an unspoken teleology that (illicitly) directs evolution along favored paths. In other words, pain and suffering are part of the package deal.

Although I agree with this conclusion, I will not spend time defending it here. What I will note, as I turn from natural evil, is that we have here a reason why I see the problem of evil as less of a problem for the Christian than many—including Darwin (and Dawkins!)—rather think. We have a version of the Leibnizian argument. Pace Voltaire, this may in fact be the best of all possible worlds. God has to work according to the rules.

Defending Darwin interlude

I want to turn now to the problem of moral evil. To do this I am going to have to rely on background science, specifically on the theory of evolution of Charles Darwin. For this reason, we had better pause for a moment. In a world of total rationality—in other words, a world where everyone thought like me—there would be no need to comment on the fact that scientifically I am as much a Darwinian as philosophically I am a Humean.

Such a world is not this world. From the first, there has been ongoing opposition from Christians, most notably those from the American South who have always opted rather for a literal reading of Genesis (Numbers 2006). It is true that they were a minority and that most people from mainline churches quickly adopted some version of evolution (Roberts 1988). This is the case today. Notably, the doctrinally and socially conservative Pope John Paul the Second (1997) explicitly endorsed, not just evolution, but a Darwinian version. Caveat emptor! Christians always want to argue that there is something special about humans and that we, unlike let us say warthogs, needed a divine intervention to complete our creation. Many Christians, in the past and today, go further and argue for continued interventions, as the deity guides the course of evolution. Notoriously, in recent years this thesis has been pushed by the so-called Intelligent Design Theorists (Dembski and Ruse 2004).

There are many fellow travelers, including, I very much regret to say, distinguished representatives of my own discipline, philosophy. Alvin Plantinga, retired now from Calvin College and Notre Dame, winner of the Templeton Prize for "affirming life's spiritual dimension," loathes and detests Darwinian theory and if at all is barely an evolutionist (Plantinga 1991, 2011). Thomas Nagel, leading American philosopher, self-proclaimed atheist, is hardly less negative about Darwinian thinking. He comments, "It seems to me that, as it is usually presented, the current orthodoxy about the cosmic order is the product of governing assumptions that are unsupported, and that it flies in the face of common sense" (2012, 5). He continues, "It is prima facie highly implausible that life as we know it is the result of a sequence of physical accidents together with the mechanism of natural selection" (Nagel 2012, 6). He asks rhetorically, "In the available geological time since the first life forms appeared on earth, what is the likelihood that, as a result of physical accident, a sequence of viable genetic mutations should have occurred that was sufficient to permit natural selection to produce the organisms that actually exist?" (Nagel 2012). Others sing the same song, notably the distinguished philosopher of mind, Jerry Fodor (with Piattelli-Palmarini 2010).

What is this Darwinian theory that I am accepting and think perfectly adequate, without need of any divine help or intervention to explain life here now and in the past? At its core is the central insight of Charles Darwin, as he argued to his mechanism of natural selection (Ruse 2008). More organisms are born than can survive and reproduce. This leads to a struggle for existence, or more pertinently reproduction. There is constant variation appearing in populations. In the struggle, some variations will aid their possessors more than other variations. There will therefore be a kind of winnowing, as the better or fit survive and reproduce and the worse or less fit lose out. Overall, there will be a natural selection, producing new features that are helpful: adaptations like the hand and the eye, the leaf and the flower. Darwin then applied this mechanism across the biological spectrum—behavior, fossils, geographical distributions, anatomy, classification, embryology. All the time, he argued that selection explains strange facts—that the embryo of human and chick are nigh identical—and in turn the explanations make more probable. This leads to the conclusion:

> It is interesting to contemplate an entangled bank, clothed with many plants of many kinds, with birds singing on the bushes, with various insects flitting about, and with worms crawling through the damp earth, and to reflect that these elaborately constructed forms, so different from each other, and dependent on each other in so complex a manner, have all been produced by laws acting around us.

He continues,

> Thus, from the war of nature, from famine and death, the most exalted object which we are capable of conceiving, namely, the production of the higher animals, directly follows. There is grandeur in this view of life, with its several powers, having been originally breathed into a few forms or into one; and that, whilst this planet has gone cycling on according to the fixed law of gravity, from so simple a beginning endless forms most beautiful and most wonderful have been, and are being, evolved. (Darwin 1859, 490–491)

There have been huge developments in Darwinian theory over the 150 years since the *Origin* was published. The basic theory holds steady. Where the big advance has come is in our far greater understanding of heredity, first thanks to the Moravian monk

Gregor Mendel, and then, after 1953 and the Watson-Crick discovery of the double helix, thanks to molecular biology applied to the problems of heredity, genetics. Natural selection working on the units of heredity, genes, is the dominant and successful paradigm. It applies also to our own species, *Homo sapiens*. Darwin knew that and so do we (Darwin 1871; Ruse 2012a). An issue of ongoing interest is whether, even if God is absent, there is any progress in evolution. In particular, were humans bound to appear? Prima facie, Darwinian theory proscribes such progress. On the one hand, the new variations appearing in populations, the building blocks of change, are random in the sense of not appearing to need. No direction there. On the other hand, although natural selection is not really a tautology—those that survive are those that survive—it is relativistic with no absolute good. Take intelligence. In the immortal words of the eminent paleontologist Jack Sepkoski: "I see intelligence as just one of a variety of adaptations among tetrapods for survival. Running fast in a herd while being as dumb as shit, I think, is a very good adaptation for survival" (Ruse 1996, 486).

For all this, prominent Darwinians, starting with Darwin himself, have thought that the theory can yield progress. Darwin appealed to what today we call biological arms races. Organisms compete against other lines, and in the process comes advance.

> If we look at the differentiation and specialisation of the several organs of each being when adult (and this will include the advancement of the brain for intellectual purposes) as the best standard of highness of organisation, natural selection clearly leads towards highness; for all physiologists admit that the specialisation of organs, inasmuch as they perform in this state their functions better, is an advantage to each being; and hence the accumulation of variations tending towards specialisation is within the scope of natural selection. (Darwin 1861, 134)

Today, Richard Dawkins buys completely into this kind of thinking. "Directionalist common sense surely wins on the very long time scale: once there was only blue-green slime and now there are sharp-eyed metazoa" (Dawkins and Krebs 1979, 508). Complementing this, we have Cambridge paleontologist Simon Conway Morris arguing that there are ecological niches, existing independently of life, that organisms seek out and occupy. He argues, "If brains can get big independently and provide a neural machine capable of handling a highly complex environment, then perhaps there are other parallels, other convergences that drive some groups towards complexity" (Morris 2003, 196). He continues, "We may be unique, but paradoxically those properties that define our uniqueness can still be inherent in the evolutionary process. In other words, if we humans had not evolved then something more-or-less identical would have emerged sooner or later" (Morris 2003).

There are other suggestions for generating progress to humans, but enough has been said. Nothing I can say here will change the thinking of the biblical literalists, the Creationists, nor experience suggests, will it change the Intelligent Design Theorists. With respect to my fellow philosophers, one would feel more confidence in the opposition if the critics showed the slightest serious knowledge of modern evolutionary science. Regrettably, lack of empirical backing has never deterred philosophers and in some circles is even taken as a sign of merit. We need not tarry. Darwinian evolutionary theory today is good and functioning science. Many think that it can generate progress to humans, but that really is another matter.[2]

Genetic determinism

Picking up now on moral evil. Where stands a skeptic like me? I have said truly that I believe in the reality of moral evil. This, I take it, implies we have choice. We have free will. A falling rock has no free will. Nor for that matter does a human who has been hypnotized. We are not rocks and generally we are not under hypnosis. We can choose. There are of course massive and ongoing philosophical debates about all of this, which we can for convenience reduce down to two (Fischer et al. 2007). When we speak of free will, do we imply that this is something that occurs within the causal nexus—"compatibilism"—or do we think it is something that escapes the causal nexus—"libertarianism." (Note that this use of "libertarian" here does not imply subscription to Ayn Rand-type economics.)

Without debate, I am going to opt here for the compatibilist position—the position of David Hume (1739–40). I do this as much for negative as for positive reasons. I realize that phenomenologically we have the feeling that we are not part of the causal nexus. Should I finish this long overdue paper or should I watch a movie? It's my choice. This said, I am really not sure what it would mean to be outside the nexus. Apart from anything else, what happens next? Do I pick up my computer or do I flick the television switch? I presume that at some point we are back in the causal nexus. How the muscles in my arms work when I pick up objects. How something triggers feelings of guilt as I slouch back into my chair and watch the credits of a golden oldie. What then triggers my reactions twenty minutes later when with regret—much regret— I turn from a wheelchair-confined Jimmy Stewart being a bit mean to Grace Kelly and focus my mind on moral non-realists and why every family needs one?[3] Positively, I am drawn to compatibilism because then it means I can bring humans beneath the pertinent scientific theories of our day. We don't have to start from scratch or blind as it were. For me, this means we can turn for guidance to the supreme theory, namely, Charles Darwin's theory of evolution through natural selection. We humans are part of the tree of life and we can apply what we know about that tree and its causes to the problems at hand. In other words, in thinking about free will and choice—and then subsequently about evil—we can do it from a Darwinian perspective.

At once, you may worry that this cannot be the way to go. Some thirty or forty years ago, when Darwinians started to think seriously about human behavior—human sociobiology or, as it has been rechristened, evolutionary psychology—the cry went up that it was fatally compromised by its commitment to "genetic determinism" (Ruse 1979; Segerstralle 1986). We are all marionettes controlled by the DNA double helix, with no more free will than Punch and Judy at the seaside. You know he is going to beat the hell out of her and he is going to get locked up by the policeman—"Hello, Hello, Hello, What's all this then?" Whatever you call it, there is not much free will here—in fact when you think about it, not much moral evil either. You may feel inclined to put down Punch like the mad dog he is—my memory of these things is that the hangman is usually waiting in the wings for his call on stage—but he is a mad dog, not a responsible human being, or puppet. Unlike Casey and Finnegan on the beloved Canadian television show for kids, *Mr. Dressup*. For a dog, Finnegan is altogether too keen on the autonomy of the will and on the Categorical Imperative.

In the years since, cooler heads have started to prevail. It is now seen that, far from an evolutionary approach locking us into universal genetic determinism, it does the very opposite! Start with the basic fact of Darwinian biology. It's all about reproduction. Far more than Freud, Darwin is into sex, sex, sex! If you don't reproduce then you are out of the game. However, as always, there is more than one way of playing the game. Indeed, as is often the case, if one group of people are playing the game one way, it might pay you to take a different strategy and play the game another way. In particular, evolutionists distinguish between what they call an r-selection-type strategy and a K-selection-type strategy. If you are living in an unstable environment, sometimes good and sometimes bad, then it might pay you to have lots of offspring with not much parental care. When the going is good, you are going to win the jackpot. However, if you are living in a relatively stable environment, it may pay to have fewer offspring, but put much parental care into their well-being.

Now think how this is going to cash out. If you are not going to look after the kids all that very much, then they had better be pretty good at doing things on their own and getting on with the job. No never-ending years as a graduate student! In other words, they had better be preprogramed to do things quickly and efficiently. Genetic determinism! Think ants. The queen has lots of offspring and, although the workers care for the young, they have to do things in their own right quickly. Not only are there no graduate programs, there is no primary, secondary, or tertiary education. Foragers are on their own from the start. The disadvantage of course is that if things go wrong, generically determined organisms cannot regroup and rethink. They get wiped out. This doesn't really matter to the queen or the nest, because there are lots more where the losers came from. So it works.

However, if organisms adopt the other strategy, with much parental care and slower growth, then you simply cannot afford to be defenseless in the face of changes and challenges. You have got to have the means to regroup and rethink. When it rains, this is disastrous for leaf cutter ants away from the nest. They are blindly following pheromone trails and if these are washed away then they are lost and helpless. Sophisticated organisms like humans cannot afford to have this happen. "How many kids do you have, Mrs. Jones?" "Three. No, two went earlier today to get a Big Mac and it has been raining. Better say one." Organisms that have gone the K-selection route have to have a dimension of freedom not possessed by the genetically determined ants.

Note that none of this takes you out of the causal nexus. Daniel Dennett (1984) is good on this. He likens r-selected organisms to simple rockets. They are cheap and plenteous. You shoot them at the target in numbers, realizing that if the target moves on they will miss. He likens K-selected organisms to complex rockets with homing devices. They are like Mars Rover. When it meets a rock or a hole, it doesn't give up. It finds a way to go around, as the complex rockets find a way to stay on target. But all of the rockets—and Mars Rover—are fully causal. It is just that the complex rockets are more expensive—as is Mars Rover. You might just decide to go quick and easy instead. Note, incidentally, that although our prime interest may be in humans, this approach certainly suggests that this is going to be a gradual phenomenon. We have more freedom than dogs, but dogs more than ants. No one expects dogs to think things through as well as humans, but they certainly do a much better job than ants. As an Englishman, I approve of that conclusion.

Moral evil

Now let us start to bring this conversation around to moral evil. One of the things that Darwinians working on behavior have always realized—it is a major topic in the *Origin*—is that much behavior is social. A lot of the time, at all levels, organisms work together for their mutual benefit. This cooperation is known technically as "altruism," but note that the implication is not that this is necessarily Mother Teresa altruism, in the sense of having a genuine concern for the welfare of others. Ants are super altruists, in the biological sense, but no one thinks that they consciously care for anyone else. That is what genetic determinism means and implies. I care blindly for the young in the nest, because if I do this my genes are more likely to be replicated. However, K-selected organisms like humans need something more. They need ways to put their biological altruism in play. This is where consciousness comes in, as people think things through. A health insurance plan is a perfect case of human altruism, at the biological level. I put into the kitty and then as needed I can withdraw. Reasoning is going to come in, for I have to make decisions about how much insurance I need to buy and so forth. I cannot afford to be genetically determined.

Now you might say that this is all very well, but what does it have to do with evil? Take buying insurance. Surely, the whole point is that this is not a moral enterprise. To use a phrase, we are selfish genes all of the way through. I don't buy insurance because I care about your well-being. I buy insurance because I care about my well-being. That is why we have debates about whether there should be state-enforced penalties for those who do not buy insurance. It is not fair if they don't buy insurance and then in times of need turn to us. That is true, but the argument now is that selfish-gene behavior, pure and simple, won't work. Apart from anything else, to make reasoned decisions takes time, and often you don't have time. The tiger is coming after my pal and me. Should I warn him? If I do, it might take the focus off him and endanger me. If I don't, he might not be around to help me when I need a lift up the tree. By the time the reasoning is over and the decision is made, we are both tiger suppers. Immanuel Kant spotted this.

> A . . . man, for whom things are going well, sees that others (whom he could help) have to struggle with great hardships, and he thinks to himself: What concern of mine is it? Let each one be as happy as heaven wills, or as he can make himself; I won't take anything from him or even envy him; but I have no desire to contribute to his welfare or help him in time of need. If such a way of thinking were a universal law of nature, the human race could certainly survive—and no doubt that state of humanity would be better than one where everyone chatters about sympathy and benevolence and exerts himself occasionally to practice them, while also taking every chance he can to cheat, and to betray or otherwise violate people's rights. (Kant [1785] 1993, 41)

Nice in theory, but as Kant saw, it wouldn't work in practice. We do need that extra shove to help us to be biological altruists.

Nature's solution was to make us genuine altruists (Ruse 1986; Ruse and Richards 2017). We do what we do because we think we

should do what we do. It is right and proper. Not to do what we
should do is wrong. This is where evil comes in. The evil person is
the person who goes against our biologically given sense of morality.
It is all perfectly natural, as you might say. However, it brings in
values: right, wrong, good, and evil. A solution, but, like all good
and powerful solutions, it raises many questions. First, do note that
no one is justifying morality at this point. We are not going from
natural, this is it, to values, this is how it should be. Hume warned
us against that.

> In every system of morality, which I have hitherto met with,
> I have always remark'd, that the author proceeds for some
> time in the ordinary way of reasoning, and establishes the
> being of a God, or makes observations concerning human
> affairs; when of a sudden I am surpriz'd to find, that instead
> of the usual copulations of propositions, *is*, and *is not*, I meet
> with no proposition that is not connected with an *ought*, or
> an *ought not*. This change is imperceptible; but is, however, of
> the last consequence. For as this *ought*, or *ought not*, expresses
> some new relation or affirmation, 'tis necessary that it shou'd
> be observ'd and explain'd; and at the same time that a reason
> should be given, for what seems altogether inconceivable, how
> this new relation can be a deduction from others, which are
> entirely different from it. But as authors do not commonly use
> this precaution, I shall presume to recommend it to the readers;
> and am persuaded, that this small attention wou'd subvert all the
> vulgar systems of morality, and let us see, that the distinction of
> vice and virtue is not founded merely on the relations of objects,
> nor is perceiv'd by reason. (Hume 1739–40, 469–70)

This is what philosopher G. E. Moore (1903) called committing the
"naturalistic fallacy," illicitly linking natural facts with nonnatural
facts, the latter including morality.

What we are doing here is strict science—explaining why we have
moral sentiments. Saying that these are adaptations, like hands and
eyes and penises and vaginas. In themselves, they have no special
status and could have been otherwise. Darwin spotted this.

It may be well first to premise that I do not wish to maintain
that any strictly social animal, if its intellectual faculties were

to become as active and as highly developed as in man, would acquire exactly the same moral sense as ours. In the same manner as various animals have some sense of beauty, though they admire widely-different objects, so they might have a sense of right and wrong, though led by it to follow widely different lines of conduct. If, for instance, to take an extreme case, men were reared under precisely the same conditions as hive-bees, there can hardly be a doubt that our unmarried females would, like the worker-bees, think it a sacred duty to kill their brothers, and mothers would strive to kill their fertile daughters; and no one would think of interfering. . . . The one course ought to have been followed, and the other ought not; the one would have been right and the other wrong. (Darwin 1871, 73–74)

With us, mothers don't generally want to kill their daughters and sisters their brothers, so what is the nature of human, evolved morality? I don't see the Darwinian saying anything very exciting here. The two best-known secular moral systems are the Kantian one—treat others as ends and not as means—and the utilitarian one—maximize happiness, minimize unhappiness. A Darwinian could and would be comfortable with both of these. Himmler was evil because he did not treat Jews as ends and he certainly did nothing to maximize their happiness. What about those notorious cases of which philosophers are so fond? If you have vital information for the allies, are you justified in bribing your guard with chocolate to let you escape? A utilitarian says yes, a Kantian says no. My suspicion is that, at a point like this, rather than there being a right answer, morality breaks down. It doesn't have an answer. I look upon this conclusion as a point of strength for me. Morality is not reading off God-given eternal truths, but working with natural adaptations. Adaptations rarely work perfectly. Ask anyone over forty about eyesight. The point is that generally we are not in concentration camps bribing guards. Generally, we are dealing with such questions as whether you, a good swimmer, should try to save a drowning child. Kantians and utilitarians agree that you should. They also agree that Hitler was a very evil man and Sophie Scholl a very good woman.

Does this mean that a Darwinian approach makes no difference to what we believe morally? Does it make no difference to what we learned in Philosophy 101 to call descriptive or normative ethics? Overall I would think—and very much hope—not. I can see some issues. What about duties to family versus duties to others, including strangers? Someone like Peter Singer (1972) would claim that we have equal duties to all. This certainly seems at times to be the position of Jesus, although whether Paul and the later followers thought the same is debatable. We certainly learn that parents have obligations to children, which are not necessarily reciprocated: "The children ought not to lay up for the parents, but the parents for the children" (2 Cor. 12:14). I suspect that for all we might say otherwise, most people feel the same. In his great novel *Bleak House*, Dickens is scathing about Mrs. Jellyby the philanthropist who spends all of her time worrying about the welfare of an African tribe, to the entire neglect of her own family, let alone the poor in her own society, like Jo the crossing sweeper. Hume knew the score,

> A man naturally loves his children better than his nephews, his nephews better than his cousins, his cousins better than strangers, where everything else is equal. Hence arise our common measures of duty, in preferring the one to the other. Our sense of duty always follows the common and natural course of our passions. (Hume 1739–40, 483–84)

Mrs. Jellyby is unnatural.

Darwinism gives us substantive morality and there is certainly a full place there for evil. Note that evil comes because of free will. However bad the actions of a person hypnotized, they are not morally evil. They could not have done otherwise. Heinrich Himmler was morally evil. He did have a choice about what he was doing. In this sense, I am inclined to agree with Christians like Alvin Plantinga (1974a), that if you have the kind of setup that we have with humans, evil is going to be as much part of the package deal as is the pain and suffering caused in the animal world by the actions of natural selection. You cannot have the one without the other. I should add parenthetically that I am not sure how far this lets God off the hook. My own sympathies lie with the chap in the *Brothers Karamazov* who felt that some evil acts were so bad that, whatever good might come eventually, nothing can excuse them and God should not have got into the creative business in the first place.

Auschwitz could never be a price worth paying. So I suppose in the end, my Darwinian non-realism is not quite as religion friendly as I am pretending.[4]

Justification

We have dealt with normative ethics. What about the 64,000-dollar question? What about justification? What about Philosophy 101 again—metaethics? Start with a couple of points. First, no one is saying that ethics is nonexistent. It may exist in the mind but it exists, just like Beethoven's fifth symphony exists and the Euler Identity—$e^{i\pi} + 1 = 0$—exists. Second, it isn't relative. Of course, it is relative to human nature, as Darwin pointed out, but realists, Christians, and others accept that too. Christians think that bestiality—sex with members of other species—is immoral. But what if we had evolved like the Amazonian Molly, that is comprised entirely of females that are parthenogenetic—need no fertilization—but that must have the stimulus first of intercourse with one of a possible four other species? Are we to understand that the pope and the Archbishop of Canterbury would forbid sexual activity outright? Obviously not. So relative to human nature, but not relative to those sharing our human nature. Sex with small children is, within the system, absolutely wrong. Himmler was an unbelievably evil man. Obviously, his great evil was made possible by modern technology, but that is another matter. Evil is evil and it exists.

What about foundations? This links us back to our Darwinian interlude. Some who are in this business of getting morality from Darwinism think that we can justify substantive morality by virtue of the fact that evolution is progressive (Wilson 1975; Richards 1986). It leads to humans. Hence, nature (contra Hume) does have value and so thoughts and behavior that promote human well-being are ipso facto good and justified. I suspect you can infer from my treatment of the biological progress question, I am not at all comfortable with this kind of move. I rush to say that I don't think it is a stupid position, even though I am not quite sure whether it still qualifies as non-realism. We all at times think nature has value (Ruse 2013). Someone who wanted to destroy the Canadian Rockies for the minerals beneath the surface would surely with good reason be accused of rape, and this implies that the Earth has value. Moreover, if you can have value for mountains, it doesn't seem silly to say you can have more value for humans. On balance though, I prefer to think of this kind of talk as metaphorical; we have powerful metaphors, but metaphors all the same.

The position I take agrees with Hume that you cannot cross the is/ought barrier and turn this into the solution (Ruse 1986). Substantive morality has no justification! It is, as I have said elsewhere, an illusion put in place by our genes to keep us good cooperators (Ruse and Wilson 1985). Note, however, what is the illusion. It is not the existence of substantive ethics. It is rather that it is objective. It doesn't just say that I don't like abuse of small children. It says that abuse of small children is wrong, absolutely. Following John Mackie (1977), I argue that we (to use his ugly word) "objectify" morality. When I say, "Killing is wrong," it is an emotion but not just an emotion. It is an emotion onto which I project the sense (or illusion) of objectivity, because if I didn't it would break down. Why should I not kill if it is all an emotion? I don't kill because I think I shouldn't, really. It truly is wrong, something outside me—bigger than all of us and hence binding on all of us. Morality is an adaptation and so also is the sense of objectivity.

Have I really refuted moral realism? I am arguing that Darwinian evolution has no fixed, absolute direction. We have evolved one way, to get our particular set of moral beliefs. We could have evolved another way, to have a different set of moral beliefs. Really, one is as good as another, so there is no reason to think that either corresponds to or found out the true objective morality. Take up the invariable objection that we sense the train bearing down on us because of our adaptations, but that does not ipso facto make the train nonreal (Nozick 1981). The situation here is different from the train bearing down on you. You might sense it by sight. You might sense it by hearing. If you are a bat, you might sense it by echolocation. All of these are adaptations. But you had better sense the train or you are dead. The thing about morality is that one system can work as well as another. There is no train to worry about. If you don't like Darwin's ant example because it seems a bit bizarre, then consider what I have called, after Eisenhower's secretary of state, the John Foster Dulles system of morality (Ruse 1986). He hated the Russians. He thought he had a moral duty to hate the Russians. But he knew that they hated him in return. So everyone got on nicely. Why should not the real morality be this rather than the morality we have about liking or loving people? It is true that everyone perhaps shares the same underlying rules of reciprocation, but, as Kant pointed out, these are not morality. Perhaps you might say that there is an objective morality out there which we may or may not have hit on through evolution. This surely gets close to being a contradiction in terms: an objective morality—perhaps the Dulles morality—of which we are totally unaware? I don't think this is what Plato or Augustine or G. E. Moore had in mind. Stay with no objective morality and that we create morality through our evolution.

I suspect that moral realists, theists and others, will be disappointed at this point—or triumphant. If this is all I mean by morality and evil then it is hardly worth considering. Himmler sent literally millions of people off to the gas chambers. He was a truly evil man. Why? Well, because he went against the will of God. He violated certain nonnatural properties, either Plato's forms or things much like them, with the status of mathematics. Religious and secular fault him because he went against that which is natural. That is what we mean by evil. It is real folks; it is real. In one sense, of course I do agree with much that is claimed here. My point is that evil does violate the natural. I think Himmler was evil because he consciously of choice went against what it is to be a full human being. Normal people don't shovel fellow humans into gas ovens. In another sense, of course I disagree entirely with what is being said here. I am breaking with the Christians and the secular moral realists—not with realism in the colloquial sense, because I think I am more realistic—and that is shocking. I think evil exists but is nonreal in this sense that it has no objective referent. This is what I mean by being a moral skeptic. But because my claim is shocking, it doesn't mean that it is wrong or that my position has no power. I am with Hume. I think that philosophy leads to skepticism—about foundations. But psychology kicks in and that, I am glad to say, is enough.

> Where am I, or what? From what causes do I derive my existence, and to what condition shall I return? Whose favour shall I court, and whose anger must I dread? What beings surround me? and on whom have I any influence, or who have any influence on me?

I am confounded with all these questions, and begin to fancy myself in the most deplorable condition imaginable, invironed with the deepest darkness, and utterly deprived of the use of every member and faculty. (Hume 1739–40, 269)

Most fortunately it happens, that since reason is incapable of dispelling these clouds, nature herself suffices to that purpose, and cures me of this philosophical melancholy and delirium, either by relaxing this bent of mind, or by some avocation, and lively impression of my senses, which obliterate all these chimeras. I dine, I play a game of backgammon, I converse, and am merry with my friends; and when after three or four hours' amusement, I would return to these speculations, they appear so cold, and strained, and ridiculous, that I cannot find in my heart to enter into them any farther. (Hume 1739–40)

Notes

1 Actually, I describe myself as atheistic about Christianity and agnostic about Ultimate Reality. I discuss my views on Christianity at length in my *Atheism: What Everyone Needs to Know* (2015) and tell more about my own position in *On Purpose* (2017b).

2 Nearly forty years ago, I stood up in federal court in Arkansas and defended Darwinian evolutionary theory against Creationism as genuine, progressive science. I have never doubted that opinion. However, for some years now I have been arguing that there is a side to the Darwinian enterprise that takes on the colors of a secular religion. It is to be found in the writings of Thomas Henry Huxley, of his grandson Julian Huxley, and most prominently recently in the writings of Edward O. Wilson. Darwinism is taken to explain the nonexistence of God, the place of humans in the cosmic scheme of things, the foundations of morality, and much more. Expectedly, Creationists have seized on this with glee claiming that I have gone over to the dark side—or rather to the light side! I have not. Darwinian theory, on which I am relying in this essay, is good professional science. Darwinism as religion is alive and well but I am not talking about it here. I do talk about it, at length, in *The Evolution-Creation Struggle* (2005), *Darwinism as Religion: What Literature Tells Us about Evolution* (2017a), and *Darwinism and War: Science or Religion?* (2018). The matter of progress to humans is an acid test. As science, Darwin thinking does not support it. As religion, it is the centerpiece of the Darwinian approach.

3 If you can identify the movie without using Google, then perhaps it
   is time for you to retire. Like the God of Job, I make the rules. I am
   seventy-seven years old, and have no intention whatsoever of retiring.

4 I am not quite as confident as I am sounding. Does the goodness of
   Sophie Scholl counter and cancel the evil of Himmler? Part of me
   wants to say yes. Part of me wants to say that, not having suffered
   myself, it is not for me to make the judgment here. I will say, still, that
   it is not the problem of evil that leads me from Jesus. I cannot get over
   the incoherence at the religion's heart.

Response to Michael Ruse

Richard Brian Davis

The "most important statement in this essay," says Michael Ruse, is that "I believe in the existence of evil. I think some people are truly evil human beings" (83). Now I don't doubt for a moment that Ruse believes these things. It's just that on "the supreme theory" (92) (i.e., his all-purpose Darwinian Naturalism (DN)) *what* Ruse believes is actually false. There is no such thing as real evil and there are no truly evil human beings. We can see this in the following ways.

First, on Ruse's view, there is no natural evil. "I don't believe in it!" (85)) he says. There are simply "unpleasant things that happen to us," (ibid.) and they are "part of the package deal" (98) if you're a Darwinist. That's fair enough. But then if evil exists at all, it will have to be *moral evil*—the sort (all too frequently) entertained or perpetrated by conscious, rational agents to deliberately cause or permit significant harm to be done to themselves or others without good reason. Clearly, to commit a moral evil, you must be a *conscious* agent. That's the bare minimum.

But here I'm at a loss to see how "the supreme theory" delivers. We're told that natural selection works on "the units of heredity," (90) accumulates variations, and ultimately produces "new features that are helpful: adaptations like the hand and the eye, the leaf and the flower" (89). No one's questioning that. The question is whether compounding these *material* parts in this *material* fashion could ever produce consciousness. It is no answer to reply, "By 'consciousness' I just mean 'the material interactions between the brain's material parts.' Evolution can explain the origin and operations of these 'neural machines.'" Certainly, but that's not what consciousness *is*.

What I'm referring to is "the reflex act by which I know that I think, and that my thought and actions are my own and not another's" (Clarke and Collins 2011, 90). *That* is accessible only through introspection. And when you carefully attend to *that* datum, it quickly becomes apparent that consciousness (in this sense) is utterly distinct from the known properties of matter. It's a different kind of thing altogether. Indeed, it is *so* different that to fancy *unconscious* brain parts could conspire together to produce a *conscious* whole brain is to forget that what you're picturing here is metaphysically impossible: that something can be produced out of nothing.[1] Thus DN commits Ruse to denying a necessary condition for there being moral evil (the only sort he believes in). The "supreme theory" therefore commits him to denying evil itself.

Second, Ruse proposes that "the reality of moral evil . . . implies we have choice. We have free will" (91). He then goes on to say that "in thinking about free will and choice—and then subsequently about evil—we can do it from a Darwinian perspective" (90). If we do that, we can see that Heinrich Himmler was morally evil because he "had a choice and he chose to kill" (84). He wasn't under hypnosis, nor was he a falling rock:

> A falling rock has no free will. Nor for that matter does a human who has been hypnotized. We are not rocks and generally we are not under hypnosis. We can choose. (91)

Or again,

> Note that evil comes because of free will. However bad the actions of a person hypnotized, they are not morally evil. They could not have done otherwise. Heinrich Himmler was morally evil. He did have a choice about what he was doing. (98)

Why wouldn't the actions of a hypnotized Himmler be morally evil? It's because (in that case) he wouldn't have a choice about what he did, which is just to say he "could not have done otherwise." Putting these ideas together, then, Ruse appears to endorse the following principle of choice. Let "S" be any agent, and let "A" be an action done by S. Then presumably, Ruse will accept,

> CHOICE: Necessarily, S had a free choice about whether to do A just in case S could have done other than A.

But once more his "supreme theory" steps in to create problems. Like Helm, Ruse is a compatibilist. He thinks free will is compatible with causal determinism. He is drawn to this view because (1) he doesn't know "what it would mean to be outside the [physical] nexus" (92). That is to say, he subscribes to the causal closure of the physical. And (2) it allows him to bring human beings and all of their features "beneath the pertinent scientific theories of our day" (ibid.).

But here we strike a problem. If we're all prisoners inside the physical nexus and everything about us is subject to scientific laws, in what sense could Himmler have done otherwise? Surely, in that case, being causally necessitated in everything he did, he *couldn't* have done otherwise; in which case, by CHOICE, he had no choice about his various atrocities. What he did, then, wasn't morally evil. Here Ruse might like to offer an analysis of "could have done otherwise" in terms of acting differently under different causes.[2] He might assert,

> CHOICE*: Necessarily, S had a free choice about whether to do A just in case (if S had been subject to different necessitating causes, S would have done other than A).

And then Ruse could declare that Himmler's evils were free on the grounds that if he had been raised in a different situation under different causes (say, in Great Britain), he would never have conceived and implemented the Final Solution.

Perhaps so, but the difficulty is that (on CHOICE*) both rocks and hypnotized Himmlers are also candidates for making free choices. If this stone could have been thrown (by me) into the water, instead of having rolled down this incline, its action would have been different than it was. But no one thinks it freely moved down the hill. Similarly, if Himmler had praised Churchill under hypnosis, no one thinks he did that freely on the grounds that if he hadn't been under hypnosis, he would have cursed Churchill instead.

The reply of course will be that rocks and hypnotized Himmlers aren't agents. So they aren't covered by CHOICE*. But *why* is that? *Why* aren't they agents? Is it because they don't author or originate their actions? That doesn't seem right; for on DN the action of everything in the causal-physical nexus is caused. Nothing has the power of initiating volitions; in which case either nothing is an agent or everything is. The problem is acute. I leave it to Ruse to clear this up. As it is, it looks as though (on DN) we either don't have free choice (so that there is no evil), or everything has choice (so that, possibly—and contra Ruse) runaway boulders and hypnotized Himmlers can be just as guilty of moral evil as you and me.

Finally, Ruse declares that "sex with small children is, within the system, absolutely wrong" (99). It is simply painful that Ruse cannot affirm this self-evident truth. I'm afraid his "supreme theory" won't have it. He must do its bidding, come what may. According to the theory, nothing is objectively evil. Of course, we believe some things *are* evil—objectively and absolutely. But this is nothing but "an illusion put in place by our genes to keep us good cooperators" (100). Sadly then, Ruse's first and "most important statement"—that there is evil—isn't factually true. The "supreme theory" knows better. The fact of the matter is,

> Darwinian evolution has no fixed, absolute direction. We have evolved one way, to get our particular set of moral beliefs. We could have evolved another way, to have a different set of moral beliefs. Really, one is as good as another. (ibid.)

Ruse says "Sex with children is absolutely wrong." He's right about that of course—absolutely right. The "supreme theory," however, won't let him say it. For DN has "no fixed, absolute direction." We could have evolved in a different way. And if we had, Ruse might well have believed "Sex with children is absolutely right," and then *that* would have been right. No less than the architect of "the supreme theory"—Darwin himself—lends his support. He writes,

> If . . . men were reared under precisely the same conditions as hive-bees, there can hardly be a doubt that our unmarried females would . . . strive to kill their fertile daughters; and no one would think of interfering. . . . The one course ought to have been followed, and the other ought not; the one would have been right and the other wrong. (cited by Ruse, 97)

That either course is objectively right (on Ruse's view) is an illusion. One course "is as good as" the other. But then if "evil" "means something with a value component," (84) we only "project the sense (or illusion)" (100) of objectivity onto our belief that Himmler was evil. Factually and objectively speaking, he wasn't. If that's what "the supreme theory" demands of us, I say so much the worse for the theory.

Paul Helm

Is Ruse a skeptic about good and evil or not? What is his skepticism exactly? The answer seems to be, if we were to ask David Hume whether one has to strike the flint to make the spark to light the cotton waste, causing a flame, he would answer yes. But he did not believe in causal necessity, that is, the existence of an objective relation between causes and effects. Rather, there are just conjunctions or counterfactuals between what we need to do to make things change in certain predictable ways. Causation functions operationally.

In a parallel way, for Ruse evils natural or moral are intramundane. There is no extramundane factor to discuss, no place for a necessary being, any more than Hume had a place for causal necessity. We observe people getting hurt by natural happenings, and by the activity of others and ourselves, and we should do our best to protect ourselves and others from their malign effects. Ruse is slimming down evil to feelings of physical pain and pleasure, caused by evolutionary changes, or that element in the effects, with no place for evil intentions. But given Ruse's Humean skepticism, he reckons that we can agree if we happen to coincide in our tastes and human habits, and as a result ethical objectivity would rest in autobiographical coincidence.

I wonder how far this Humean skepticism that Ruse professes reaches. Presumably for him there are no objective morally good or bad states, except the products of physical change. Also, are our moral views the product of the operation of the passions, not of the reason? It is rather like ice cream. For me vanilla is good, but for you chocolate. So we can differ in our choices, and never disagree. There is no fact of the matter about the goodness of ice cream flavors, no such thing as unqualifiedly good ice cream. Moral distinctions are not derivable from reason.

Ruse and I have nothing in common here, except where we agree on the desirability of policies which, having similar tastes, we may agree are desirable attempts to ameliorate the effects of "evil," though that is not the chief thing for a Christian. On Christianity, in thinking that the sayings and actions of Jesus the Galilean were nastily theologized by Paul the Apostle, Ruse is firmly Harnackian. (There are some value-judgments lurking here, I guess, but we'll leave them alone.)

I don't think there is the dislocation that Ruse imagines between the eternal God and the God who reveals himself in time and who is incarnate in his Son. John the Apostle does quite a good job to harmonize the two in his Prologue to his Gospel (Jn. 1) and the New Testament in general. All the same, having harmonized as best as we can, we are left with a sense of mystery, provoked by events having taken place that were necessarily without parallel in human experience as, to take the classic instance, in the incarnation.

Since it is a point of some importance, a word about what Ruse tells us about total depravity. It is certainly a Calvinist term, but it does not entail that "all of the time" (83). It asserts that the effects of sin touch each of the elements in the human mind: the intellect, the will, and the emotions. All are warped and disordered. The depravity is total in that sense. Those who have held and who hold to this realistic, even if not immediately uplifting, position also recognize civil virtue, human kindness, sympathy, and so on. Looking around at the often romantic, sentimental alternatives, this is hardly an outlandish claim. And Jonathan Edwards's infamous words make a basic point of our human lot, that we may die suddenly, and in doing so, we meet our Maker. This is necessarily primitive talk for those who do not believe we are created. Of course, we can recognize that these remarks early on in his piece are part of Ruse's softening up of his readers, ridding them of the influence of as many of what he sees are the evils of the Christian religion in one of its most serious expressions, Calvinism.

So far there have been no arguments, and no attempt at an explanation of evil. I suppose for a kind of skeptic, the explanation of evil should be largely a sociological one. These people have reasons R1 for holding their views on evil, and my sort of people, who have different views, have reasons R2, where reasons are causes. These are the terms of the analysis of an argument with these assumptions, which certainly avoid stupidity.

However, these initial sentiments about skepticism are not sustained throughout Ruse's piece. In making a sketch of Darwinism, which he avows, Ruse unskeptically believes in the reality of moral evil (83) which implies that we have choice (as distinct from being subject to nothing but natural evils). Ruse seems to have a firmer hold on good and evil once the scaffolding of genetic universalism is in place. On the question of free will, which he suddenly introduces on page 91, he opts for a materialistic compatibilism which for him has the advantage that men and women can be scientifically examined. So by this stage, maybe Ruse's position amounts overall to a kind of ethical pluralism in which moral good and evil have an objectivity within communities, or disciplines—the body of genetic materialists being one such community, the materialism of Marxists being another, the dualism of traditional Christians another, and so on. Between some of these groups there may be considerable overlap, hardly any between others, though there may be some commonality at the level of public policy about what sorts of behavior ought to be penalized or rewarded.

So, it seems that Darwinism erects the scaffolding back on which to develop an account of moral realism, explaining why we have moral sentiments, and discoursing on the moral sentiments that we in fact have. So the senses of goodness and wickedness used in the context of Darwinism seem, despite the initial skepticism that Ruse professes, fairly robust, in a "good-for-me, but maybe not good-for-you" sense. Darwinism is constructed in the sense in which, early in his piece Ruse says that religion is made up, that is to say, it is a human construction as is religion. There is skepticism about Darwinianism afoot, as the work of, say, Fodor, Nagel, and Plantinga show. It is falsifiable, not like Euclidianism. But Darwinism, being credible to Ruse, delivers objective senses of good and evil for him. (This is Darwinism considered more as a religion than what is confined to observation and experiment.) Without a traditional view of creation there is a sort of convergence between biological sophistication and those religious thinkers, like for instance George Lindbeck (1984) for whom Christian doctrine is built on "community" or "forms of life."

But surprisingly, moving up the genetic scale, Ruse suddenly avows in the case of humans, "a dimension of freedom," which nevertheless remains within the causal nexus (94). I could not discern an argument. He reaches for Daniel Dennett to help him at this point.

Note that none of this takes you out of the causal nexus. Daniel Dennett (1984) is good on this. He likens r-selected organisms to simple rockets. They are cheap and plenteous. You shoot them at the target in numbers, realizing that if the target moves on they will miss. He likens K-selected organisms to complex rockets with homing devices. (94)

But those organisms characterized as rockets are not apt to mechanistic determinism, but are to be understood teleologically, in terms of chosen ends and means, surely an un-Darwinian thought if taken literally. Even robotic rockets will have had a human purpose in their history.

We see then that for Ruse moral goodness and moral evil are social notions. He does not give much time to the inner selves of moral agents, motivations, self-deception, weakness of will, or the workings of conscience. This is in sharp contrast to how these notions figure strongly in the moral outlook of Christians; "For as a man thinks in his heart so is he" (Prov 23:7). There is more to life than strategies of reproduction, which explains the cardinal virtue of altruism, Hume's sympathy. This mono-explanation, or family of them, looks a poor candidate as an explanation of the range and multiplicity of evils. It also is insufficient for trying to persuade us that there is more to morality than legality. But Ruse is content with such "substantive morality" (108). He candidly states that he thinks that morality comes from the progressive character of evolution, while being frank that he is "not at all comfortable with this kind of move" (99). Trading on the ambiguity of "nature gets better," this looks to be begging the question. Earlier, Ruse had distanced himself from those "prominent Darwinians, [who], starting with Darwin himself, have thought that the theory can yield progress" (90). But in fact these verdicts are the ones Ruse comes to hold to, noting the warning of his earlier discomfort and siding with Hume that "is" does not imply "ought." A skeptic still?

Erik J. Wielenberg

The word "morality" can mean two quite different things. Sometimes "morality" refers to certain psychological and/or social phenomena—human moral *beliefs, emotions, or practices*; other times, "morality" refers to objective moral *truths or facts*. My belief that it's morally wrong to torture babies just for fun is part of morality in the first sense; the fact that such torture actually is morally wrong (if there is such a fact) is part of morality in the second sense. Relatedly, explaining morality in the first sense is an entirely different project from explaining morality in the second sense. Just as it is one thing to explain *my belief* that Napoleon was defeated at Waterloo and something entirely different to explain Napoleon's defeat at Waterloo, similarly it is one thing to explain *my belief* that torturing babies for fun is morally wrong and something entirely different to explain the actual wrongness of torturing babies just for fun.

Ruse accepts that morality in the first sense exists but denies that morality in the second sense exists, and he sketches an evolutionary explanation of morality in the first sense. Well into that explanation he remarks that "no one is justifying morality at this point. . . . What we are doing here is strict science. Explaining why we have moral sentiments" (96). That passage indicates that Ruse is offering an evolutionary explanation for human moral beliefs, emotions, and practices rather than an explanation or account of any moral facts. Ruse's rejection of the reality of objective moral facts comes out most clearly when he says that the objectivity of ethics is "an illusion put in place by our genes to keep us good cooperators" (100). He explains further that "the existence of substantive ethics" is not an illusion; rather, the illusion is that substantive ethics is objective (ibid.). When Ruse says that substantive ethics exists, he is affirming the existence of certain ethical beliefs and emotions common to all human beings—morality in the first sense. And when he says that the objectivity of ethics is an illusion, he is denying the existence of morality in the second sense. Ruse, then, is a nihilist: he thinks that evolution can explain why we believe that certain things are morally right or wrong, good or evil, but that nothing really is morally right or wrong, good or evil.

At various points in his essay, Ruse asserts that evil exists. Such passages can, understandably, obscure the fact that Ruse thinks that evil does not exist. When Ruse says that evil exists, what he means is something like "things that are generally classified by humans as evil exist." Ruse's declarations of the existence of evil carry with them an implicit qualifier—something like "according to shared human moral beliefs." At one point Ruse makes this qualifier explicit, writing: "Sex with small children is, *within the system*, absolutely wrong" (113; emphasis added).

As far as I can tell, Ruse offers one main argument for his denial of the existence of objective ethical truths, an argument based on the alleged contingency of human moral beliefs and emotions:

> I am arguing that Darwinian evolution has no fixed, absolute direction. We have evolved one way, to get our particular set of moral beliefs. We could have evolved another way, to have a different set of moral beliefs. Really, one is as good as another, so there is no reason to think that either corresponds to or found out the true objective morality. (100)

I take it that the thought here is that there is a wide range of diverse sets of moral beliefs that evolutionary forces might have instilled in us and that it is just a matter of chance that we ended up with the particular moral beliefs that we happen to have. Therefore, even if there are objective ethical facts out there, it's unlikely that our moral beliefs correspond with such facts.

In thinking about this argument, it is important to keep in mind that if there are objective moral facts, the most basic of them are necessary truths.[3] Therefore, if there is any improbability in the correspondence between our psychological dispositions and moral reality, it must lie entirely on the psychological side of the equation. Consider the fact that we are disposed to reason in accordance with the law of noncontradiction; such reasoning often leads us to the truth. How lucky are we to arrive at such truths? Since it couldn't have been the case that the law of noncontradiction is false, it can't be that our luck lies in that principle being true. Thus, the important question is: how probable is it that we would be disposed to reason in accordance with the law of noncontradiction? Whether Ruse's argument succeeds therefore depends on the answer to the following question: to what extent do the actual laws of nature permit the emergence of beings that form their moral judgments in accordance with general principles radically different from the moral principles that shape our judgments?

Suppose for the sake of argument that there is what Ruse calls "the true objective morality." Consider the set of all necessarily true general moral principles; call that set Moral Truth. Suppose for the sake of argument that the following claim is true:

> Extreme Specificity (ES): *The actual laws of nature entail that any being capable of forming moral beliefs forms such beliefs in accordance with all and only the principles included in Moral Truth.*

Now, ES is plainly false; the existence of actual variation in human moral belief shows that the laws of nature permit a certain degree of variation in human moral beliefs. But the point I want to make does not depend on ES being true.

Imagine someone, Margaret, who is capable of forming moral beliefs and hence, on the assumption that ES is true, forms her moral judgments in accordance with all and only the principles included in Moral Truth. Notice that the obtaining of the actual laws of nature is either metaphysically necessary or metaphysically contingent. Still assuming ES to be true for the sake of argument, let's consider both options. If the laws of nature are metaphysically necessary, then given ES, it follows that

> Metaphysical Extreme Specificity (MES): *It's metaphysically necessary* that any being capable of forming moral beliefs forms such beliefs in accordance with all and only the principles included in Moral Truth.

Given MES, there is no improbability at all in the fact that Margaret forms her moral judgments in accordance with true moral principles since the correspondence between her moral beliefs and moral reality is metaphysically necessary. Suppose, on the other hand, that the laws of nature are metaphysically contingent. Still assuming the truth of ES, it follows that

> Nomological Extreme Specificity: *It is nomologically necessary but metaphysically contingent that* any being capable of forming moral beliefs forms such beliefs in accordance with the principles included in Moral Truth.

Here, perhaps, there is room for a certain sort of improbability in the fact that Margaret's moral judgments conform with true moral principles. There are metaphysically possible worlds in which the laws of nature are different from those in the actual world; in some of those worlds, Margaret judges in accordance with false moral principles. However, notice that given our assumptions, most (if not all) of our knowledge depends on just the same sort of improbability (see Enoch 2011, 173). For just as there are metaphysically possible worlds where Margaret judges in accordance with false moral principles and so lacks moral knowledge, similarly there are metaphysically possible worlds where the laws of nature are such that there is a causal process that continuously generates massively deceived brains-in-vats with mental lives indistinguishable from our own. Thus, given our assumptions, Margaret is no luckier in possessing moral knowledge than she is in possessing any other sort of knowledge.

Of course, ES is false. But ES lies at one end of a continuum, and the closer we are to ES, the less improbability there is in the correspondence between our moral beliefs and objective moral reality. So, the crucial question is, how close are we to ES? As far as we know, the actual laws of nature are such that the only way beings with the sort of cognitive complexity required to form moral beliefs can arise is by way of evolutionary processes. Accordingly, let us consider the following question: could evolutionary processes operating within the constraints of the actual laws of nature produce beings that form moral beliefs in accordance with moral principles *radically* different from the principles that guide our moral beliefs? There is some reason to think that the answer is no. It takes a lot of cognitive complexity to form moral beliefs—the sort of cognitive complexity that plausibly requires an extended developmental period during which the moralizer-to-be is relatively helpless. Thus, babies of the only species known to form moral beliefs are, as Robert Wright memorably puts it, "mounds of helpless flesh: tiger bait" (1994, 58). Consequently, it's plausible that the young of such moralizing species require extended periods of care from multiple caregivers, not just their mothers—an idea explored in depth by anthropologist Sarah Hrdy (2009). The human phenomenon of the pair bond as well as the need for mothers to enlist the help of "alloparents" (Hrdy 2009) in child-raising is associated with a host of psychological dispositions that are absent in other species— psychological dispositions that surely influence our moral cognition. These considerations are hardly decisive, but they indicate that it is a mistake simply to assume that it is nomologically possible for us (or other beings) to have evolved to form moral judgments in accordance with radically different moral principles than the ones that in fact guide our moral judgments. Again, this is not to say that ES is true—there clearly is actual variation in human moral beliefs. But there is reason to be skeptical that human moral beliefs could have been radically different than they are. And so there is reason to be skeptical of Ruse's contingency argument for nihilism.

Notes

1 For argument details, see my lead essay in Chapter 4 of this volume.

2 This analysis is suggested by Ruse's claim that the causal nexus could have been different, since "we could have evolved another way" (100).

3 The argument that follows is drawn from chapter 4 of Wielenberg 2014.

Reply to Critics

Michael Ruse

Richard Brian Davis

Well, I hate to have to use this kind of language, but Richard Davis and I seem simply to be in different paradigms. I am sure he is a very nice chap and I think of myself as a nice chap, but there we are with two nice chaps staring at each other across the divide, simply unable to bridge. Simply unable to hear what the other chap is saying, although I am sure Davis is like me in thinking: "I hear what he says, alright, and I don't like it."

It boils down to this supreme theory business. On the one hand, we have my position—as Davis rightly says, Darwinian naturalistic turtles all of the way down (or up). On the other hand, we have a more recognizable philosophical position—one where we distinguish reasons from causes, where free will is not simply a matter of laws in motion, and where in some sense morality is human-independent, absolute. What Heinrich Himmler did was wrong, even if there is no one left in the ghetto to watch him.

I am just not sure how much further we can go. Although I will say this, that I recognize the picture Davis presupposes—I don't want unfairly to put words into his mouth, so let me just say "my usual critic" presupposes—is the picture of common sense. Moreover, it is a rather nicer position than the nigh-cynical position I endorse and promote. So let me also say that, as a former believer in this position, I continue to take it very seriously. I must explain it, as indeed I do. I argue that it is an adaptive illusion because, if we didn't have it, we wouldn't function as well as social animals. This, incidentally, is all cause and effect. We developed a moral system and moved to extreme sociality, because the one spurred the other and conversely. Our lack or loss of serious fighting tools—teeth, physical strength, tiger-like aggression—not to mention concealed ovulation—are all part of the package deal. Imagine trying to teach a philosophy class with one of your students in heat. You may not be comfortable with this conclusion—emotionally I am not entirely comfortable with it myself—but it is true. Grownups opt for the truth, however painful.

Paul Helm

Paul Helm and I are on the same page on this recognition of stark differences. What is interesting for me is that—as I think he should—he ties all of this in with Christianity.

> Ruse and I have nothing in common here, except where we agree on the desirability of policies which, having similar tastes, we may agree are desirable attempts to ameliorate the effects of "evil," though that is not the chief thing for a Christian. On Christianity, in thinking that the sayings and actions of Jesus the Galilean were nastily theologized by Paul the Apostle, Ruse is firmly Harnackian. (109)

Well, I don't know about Harnack, although I trust that the reference is not to his appalling behavior in the First World War. I am with Karl Barth on this. I am firmly Quaker, the religion in which I was raised in the first twenty years of my life. The literal existence of Adam and Eve were irrelevant to my religion and I have always felt fighting Creationism to be a moral duty. This has always been combined with total literalism about the Sermon on the Mount. I remember my horror when first I learned it was not an actual transcription of a sermon given one Sunday afternoon in Northern Israel, but was more likely a compilation put together by Peter or his followers to shove it to Paul.

I do think that, beneath the levity and personal reminiscence, there is an important point. If we divide, as I think we can, moral inquiry into substantive ethics—what should I believe?—and metaethics—why should I believe what I should believe?—then general opinion (mine for a long time) is that naturalists like me and nonnaturalists opposed to me are going to be way apart on metaethics but close or identical on substantive ethics. Even as we disagree about foundations, we both agree that you ought not use yellow marker all over the books you have borrowed from the library.

More and more though, I am starting to think that perhaps we are separated at both levels. At the substantive level, nonnaturalists might be believing things that someone like me thinks not just wrong but morally undesirable. I wrote in my main essay about the differential nature of morality for the naturalist. I just don't think it moral to treat your own children indifferently, as if they were no more to you than unknown kids in Africa. Of course, you know you are going to treat your kids differently, but that is because you love them. But is this moral? I argue that it is. I am not sure that a Christian should though.

At least, I would like to have seen this spelled out in the Sermon on the Mount. As it is, things strike me as ambiguous. On the one hand, we learn "But if any provide not for his own, and specially for those of his own house, he hath denied the faith, and is worse than an infidel" (1 Tim. 5:8). On the other hand, there is Jesus: "If any man come to me, and hate not his father, and mother, and wife, and children, and brethren, and sisters, yea, and his own life also, he cannot be my disciple" (Lk. 14:26). Pay your money and take your choice, but I do sense that sometimes what Jesus says simply does not ring true with what we intuitively think is right. After his death, his followers quickly set about cleaning things up. I would go on to say that it is a pity that so much of the cleanup was done by two who had such severe sexual hang-ups—Saints Paul and Augustine.

I am a little surprised that Paul Helm labels me a progressivist (111) who thinks that this justifies morality. I express sympathy for the position. It does not strike me as an immediately bad or stupid thing to say. I truly do think that the present US administration has put in place policies that will lead to the rape of the environment— and if that isn't showing value about or in the physical world, I don't know what is. That said, I make it clear that on balance I think this kind of talk is best construed as metaphorical. The environment is something that *we* value, ultimately. I don't think that this implies—as Edward O Wilson thinks it implies—that such value must be utilitarian, like—"Don't kill off unknown species, because down the road they might yield new medicines and so forth." I think one can have a kind of aesthetic value seeing value in the things themselves—where you apparently are imputing value to things. Ultimately, though, I stand with Hume—"is" and "ought" are different things and must be seen as such. I should add parenthetically I am very dubious about biological progress. I would much rather be a human than a warthog, but warthogs thrive very nicely in conditions that would, literally, be the death of me.

Erik J. Wielenberg

When I turn to Erik J. Wielenberg's response to me, I feel that I am back at Square One. Here we go again. "At various points in his essay Ruse asserts that evil exists. Such passages can, understandably, obscure the fact that Ruse thinks that evil does not exist" (112). Well, all I can say is—"News to me!" I do think that the main move that Wielenberg makes against me is dicey. I worry about an objective morality that has no effect on our behavior—about which we may be entirely ignorant. To me this is a kind of contradiction in terms. Wielenberg makes the kind of move I would make—we are fallible and sometimes get things wrong.

Yes, but. Surely, if you have objective morality, it is going to impress itself on you. You don't have to be a Calvinist to know that there must be something like a *sensus divinitatis* about this all. Of course, Christians think this all got messed up by the apple-eating actions of Adam and original sin and the truth now being hidden from us. I have the suspicion that Wielenberg doesn't want to go down this path; he wants me hung by my own petard and this is certainly not my petard. In any case, it is false, because Darwinian evolutionary theory shows without any shadow of a doubt that Adam and Eve simply didn't exist.

From my viewpoint, it is worse than that. If someone makes a mistake about a mathematical truth, you can correct them in such a way that they take the correction as proper. They can be shown the error of their ways. It is the same with morality really. I think we should do one thing—say enact universal state-supported medicine—and you think the other—let the free market provide. At least in theory, we have a chance of reconciliation. For instance, the solution of Mitt Romney when he was governor of Massachusetts—don't compel people to buy insurance, but make them pay a penalty if they don't.

I am suggesting something more radical. Go back to Darwin and those worker bees: they have "a sacred duty to kill their brothers, and mothers would strive to kill their fertile daughters; and no one would think of interfering. . . . The one course ought to have been followed, and the other ought not; the one would have been right and the other wrong" (1871, 73–74). I just don't see anything Wielenberg says that touches this. Objective morality might be completely different, the sort of stuff we believe. But who in the ant world could go there (or, rather, come here)? It would be like you telling me that—and I am trying to think of something so disgustingly absurd that you must get my point—I ought to eat feces twice a day because that is what is demanded of us. Why? I am not a dung beetle, nor do I think it would be a good way to deal with the sanitation issues that we face. I just don't see any way of bridging the gap on this—which is my point. Objective morality could well be cut off from us because of the way we have evolved. Unfortunately, that is just not an option for objective morality.

I have said enough. We have probably all said enough. It is now time for the reader to jump into the conversation. That is the reason for this book and why I wanted to contribute. Like Saint Paul and those epistles, I am in for the long haul.

4

Evil and Atheistic Moral Realism

Erik J. Wielenberg

Evil is both ubiquitous and multifarious. James Waller observes that "in virtually every human culture, there has existed some word for 'evil,' a linguistic acknowledgement of its reality in everyday human affairs" (2007, 10). Among the kinds of things that can be evil are states of affairs, actions, intentions, and persons. Alex, the young protagonist of Anthony Burgess's novel *A Clockwork Orange*, intentionally engages in acts of extreme violence for the sake of the pleasure he derives from such acts. As he puts it: "What I do I do because I like to do" (Burgess 1988, 47). Similarly, the young Augustine steals pears for the sake of the pleasure he derives from such acts. As he puts it, "I loved evil solely because it was evil" ([400] 1993, 29). When Alex and his friends beat up an old man for the fun of it, evil states of affairs (e.g., that the old man suffers), evil actions (e.g., the beating), evil intentions (e.g., to beat the old man just for the sake of pleasure), and evil persons (e.g., Alex) are exemplified.

But what is it for something to be evil? Part of the answer to that question, I believe, is that for something to be evil is for there to be a reason to avoid or eliminate the thing.[1] I do not claim that this is all there is to being evil, but it is one important element of evil. If this is right, then evil has a normative component. To understand this normative component better, consider Derek Parfit's distinction between *normative* and *motivating* reasons (2011a, 37).[2]

Parfit explains that "facts give us [normative] reasons . . . when they count in favour of our having some attitude, or acting in some way" (2011a, 31). The fact that the cheesecake before me is delicious counts in favor of my eating it; this cheesecake fact gives me a normative reason to eat the cheesecake. Parfit illustrates that we can have conflicting normative reasons with this simple example: "If I enjoy walnuts, this fact gives me a reason to eat them; but, if they would kill me, this fact gives me a stronger or weightier conflicting reason *not* to eat them" (2011a, 32). Parfit also claims that we can have normative reasons of which we are unaware:

> Suppose that, while walking in some desert, you have disturbed and angered a poisonous snake. You believe that, to save your life, you must run away. In fact you must stand still, since this snake will attack only moving targets. . . . You have no [normative] reason to run away, and a decisive [normative] reason *not* to run away.[3] (2011a, 34)

Motivating reasons, by contrast, are psychological states that actually motivate people to act in certain ways. And of course normative and motivating reasons can diverge: "If you ran away from the angry snake, your motivating reason would be provided by your false belief that this act would save your life. But . . . you have no normative reason to run away. You merely think you do" (Parfit 2011a, 37).

The evil of Augustine's act of stealing pears and Alex's act of beating up the old man consists in part in there being normative reasons to refrain from performing these actions. Normative reasons are defeasible in that it is possible for them to be outweighed by other normative reasons. However, in the particular case of these actions, it seems that there are no outweighing normative reasons in favor of performing the acts and hence they ought not be performed, all things considered.

Normative reasons are objective features of reality—objective in the sense identified by Michael Huemer. Huemer contrasts objectivity with subjectivity, which he defines thusly:

> F-ness is subjective = Whether something is F constitutively depends at least in part on the psychological attitude or response that observers have or would have toward that thing.[4] (Huemer 2005, 2)

For example, "Funniness is subjective, because whether a joke is funny depends on whether people would be amused by it" (Huemer 2005, 2). Huemer notes that happiness is objective in his sense because "whether a person is happy depends on the attitude of someone—namely, the person himself—but it does not depend upon the attitudes of *observers towards* him" (Huemer 2005, 3). A property is objective just in case it is not subjective. So, the fact that there is a normative reason for Alex not to beat up the old man does not depend at all on the psychological attitude or response that observers would have toward the act and hence is objective. This normative reason is out there in the world.

Many thinkers have found the notion that reality includes objective normative reasons of the sort just described puzzling or implausible. If evil has the normative component I have claimed that it does, then those same thinkers will find the notion that reality includes evil puzzling or implausible. These considerations point toward the existence of what might be called the *metaphysical* problem of evil, which can be contrasted with what might be called the *theological* problem of evil. To get a sense of the difference between these two problems of evil, consider the difference between accounting for the presence of a monolith (a) within territory controlled by a very wise and powerful king who despises monoliths and (b) on the surface of the moon (as in Stanley Kubrick's film *2001: A Space Odyssey*). In case (a) what needs to be explained is how the monolith is there despite the apparent presence of an entity that has the means and desire to prevent the monolith from being there, whereas in case (b) what needs to be explained is how the monolith is there despite the apparent absence of any entity that could have produced it. Case (a) parallels the theological problem of evil, whereas case (b) parallels the metaphysical problem of evil. My aim in the remainder of this chapter is to address the metaphysical problem of evil.

Nonnatural ethical properties and basic ethical facts

Broadly speaking, there are three main options for those who hold that at least some ethical properties (like the property of there being an objective normative reason to avoid or eliminate such-and-such) are objective properties: naturalism, supernaturalism, and nonnaturalism. According to naturalism, ethical properties are, at bottom, natural properties of some sort or another (see, for example, Brink 1989). On this view, the ethical just is the natural. According to supernaturalism, ethical properties are, at bottom, supernatural properties of some sort or another. Robert Adams has advanced a rich and sophisticated version of supernaturalism (1999). On Adams's view, the ethical just is the divine. Although naturalism and supernaturalism are strikingly different in some respects, they are importantly alike in that they are both reductive in nature, declaring that ethical properties ultimately turn out to be properties of some other kind.

I am skeptical of both naturalism and supernaturalism. To understand the reasons for my skepticism, it will be helpful to consider an oft-told metaethical tale.[5] It goes like this. Back in the early twentieth century, G. E. Moore advanced his influential open question argument. Legend has it that this argument aimed to show that goodness was neither identical with nor reducible to any other property, and the reasoning is said to have gone something like this: consider any property, N, that goodness is allegedly identical with or reducible to. A question of the form, I know that x is N—but is x good? is always open; the answer is never trivially yes—as it would be if goodness were identical with or reducible to N.[6] This argument seemed decisive until certain advances in the philosophy of language taught us that identity among properties is not always transparent; some properties have a hidden nature that cannot be revealed through conceptual analysis alone. A classic example is the property of being water. It turns out that the property of *being water* is identical with the property of *being H_2O*—but this identity is not one that can be discovered through conceptual analysis alone. For those unfamiliar with the relevant science, questions of the form, I know that x is water—but is it H_2O? are open; nevertheless, *being water* = *being H_2O*. Therefore, it is argued, something similar could be the case with respect to an ethical property like *being evil*. That property might have a hidden nature; it could turn out to be identical with or reducible to a natural or supernatural property in something like the way that *being water* turned out to be identical with *being H_2O*.

It seems to me that the moral of this metaethical tale offers far less hope for the plausibility of naturalism or supernaturalism than is sometimes thought. While I agree that the example of water and H_2O shows that not all claims of identity can be accurately evaluated from the armchair, it remains the case that some identity claims can be reasonably and confidently rejected from the armchair. Huemer offers the following example:

> Suppose a philosopher proposes that the planet Neptune is Beethoven's Ninth Symphony. I think we can see that that is false, simply by virtue of our concept of Neptune and our concept of symphonies. Neptune is an entirely different kind of thing from Beethoven's ninth symphony. No further argument is needed. (2005, 94; see also Parfit 2011b, 324–25)

We can acknowledge that the properties *being a planet* and *being a symphony* may have natures that are partially hidden from us, not accessible from the armchair, and yet reasonably remain confident that nothing in their hidden nature is compatible with the claim that some planets are symphonies. Similarly, it seems to me that at least some ethical properties are entirely different kinds of things from natural or supernatural properties and that naturalism and supernaturalism "secure the 'reality' of ethical facts and properties only by turning them into something else and deflating them in the process" (2008, 159).[7] In particular, it seems to me that the property of there *being an objective normative reason to avoid or eliminate such-and-such* is of a fundamentally different type than any natural or supernatural property, and hence *being evil* is neither a natural nor a supernatural property. It is primarily for this reason that I hew to a view that has come to be known as *robust normative realism*. David Enoch characterizes robust normative realism as follows: "There are response-independent, nonnatural, irreducibly normative truths . . . objective ones, that when successful in our normative inquiries we discover rather than create or construct" (Enoch 2007, 21). On this view, normative properties are sui generis, a fundamental type of property not reducible to or fully constituted by some other type of property.

Although my view is nonnaturalistic in that it posits the existence of nonnatural properties, I think that naturalistically inclined philosophers need not necessarily be troubled by this aspect of my view. To see this, it will be helpful to consider David Chalmers's discussion of the relationship between naturalism and his views on qualia.

Qualia are phenomenal properties or the "what-it's-like" aspects of conscious experience (see Chalmers 1996, 6–11 for a useful "catalog" of various qualia). Chalmers argues that qualia are not reducible to physical processes; instead, they are sui generis. He claims that a completed theory of physics "is not *quite* a theory of everything. To bring consciousness within the scope of a fundamental theory, we need to introduce *new* fundamental properties and laws" (1996, 126). Chalmers labels his view "naturalistic dualism" and offers the following explanation of the label: "It is naturalistic because it posits that everything is a consequence of a network of basic properties and laws, and because it is compatible with all the results of contemporary science" (1996, 128). Later, he writes,

> Nothing about the dualist view I advocate requires us to take the physical sciences at anything other than their word. The causal closure of the physical is preserved; physics, chemistry, neuroscience, and cognitive science can proceed as usual. In their own domains, the physical sciences are entirely successful. They explain physical phenomena admirably; they simply fail to explain conscious experience. . . . to deny materialism is not to deny naturalism. A naturalistic dualism expands our view of the world, but it does not invoke the forces of darkness. (1996, 170)

My brand of robust normative realism is naturalistic at least to the extent that Chalmers's naturalistic dualism is. Like Chalmers, I endorse the existence of nonphysical properties but do not reject the causal closure of the physical or deny that the physical sciences are entirely successful in their own domains. If naturalistic dualists can get by without invoking the forces of darkness, then so can robust normative realists.[8]

I turn now to another important element of my metaethical view: a commitment to the existence of what I call *basic ethical facts*. The ensuing discussion of this aspect of my view will reveal some important similarities between my view and certain commitments central to traditional theism.

I take it that a fundamental category of existing things is the category of *states of affairs*. States of affairs are necessarily existing abstract entities that obtain or fail to obtain. *Facts* are obtaining or actual states of affairs; among these, some are contingent, meaning they obtain in some but not all metaphysically possible worlds, whereas others are necessary, meaning they obtain in all metaphysically possible worlds (see Plantinga 1974b, 2, 44–45). The state of affairs in which Alvin Plantinga is a philosopher obtains contingently; the state of affairs in which Alvin Plantinga is not identical to the number two obtains necessarily. Among states of affairs that obtain necessarily, some are relatively uninteresting in that the sentences that express them are devoid of substantive content. The state of affairs in which all bachelors are unmarried may fall into this category. But other necessary states of affairs are not trivial in this way. Many theists maintain that the state of affairs in which God exists is a substantive, interesting state of affairs that holds in all metaphysically possible worlds (see Plantinga 1974b, 215–16).

Some facts obtain because of the obtaining of other states of affairs. Consider, for example, the fact that the bottle of water in my office is suspended about four feet from the surface of the earth. This state of affairs obtains because another state of affairs obtains—namely, that the bottle is sitting on the surface of the desk in my office (other states of affairs—e.g., states of affairs involving gravity—also play an explanatory role here). Some states of affairs that obtain are what we may call *brute facts*; their obtaining is not explained by the obtaining of other states of affairs. Bruteness is an ontological rather than epistemological concept; that a given fact is brute does not imply that it cannot be proven or inferred from other things one knows. Theists typically maintain that the fact that God exists is a brute fact. As Richard Swinburne puts it, "No other agent or natural law or principle or necessity is responsible for the existence of God. His existence is an ultimate brute fact" (1977, 267; see also Plantinga 2011, 28). Many such theists also maintain that God exists necessarily. There is, therefore, a tradition in monotheism according to which the fact that God exists is a substantive, metaphysically necessary, brute fact.

Some states of affairs involve ethical properties, properties like moral rightness, moral wrongness, goodness, evil, virtue, vice, and the like. Some ethical states of affairs obtain; indeed, some of them obtain necessarily. Consider, for instance, the fact that pain's natural intrinsic properties make it intrinsically evil. These states of affairs obtain not just in the actual world but in all metaphysically possible worlds (see Parfit 2011a, 129).

Other ethical states of affairs hold contingently. For instance, suppose that by pushing a certain button I would knowingly torture an innocent person just for fun. This means that it is wrong for me to push the button, but this state of affairs holds contingently because there are possible worlds in which my pushing the button would not have such a nefarious result. Moreover, at least some necessarily obtaining brute ethical facts are not trivial but substantive (see Moore 1903, 7, 143); I think this is true of the pain example given above. Therefore, my view has an ontological commitment shared by many theists: it implies the obtaining of substantive, metaphysically necessary, brute facts. Some ethical facts fall into this category; I call such facts *basic ethical facts*. Such facts are the foundation of (the rest of) objective morality and rest on no foundation themselves. To ask of such facts, "Where do they come from?" or "On what foundation do they rest?" is misguided in much the way that, according to many theists, it is misguided to ask of God, "Where does He come from?" or "On what foundation does He rest?" The answer is the same in both cases: they come from nowhere, and nothing external to themselves grounds their existence; rather, they are fundamental features of the universe that ground other truths.

This point is important because both theists and non-theists alike have claimed that if there is no God, then ethics lacks an external foundation and therefore is in some sense illusory. On the theistic side, William Lane Craig declares that "in a universe without God, good and evil do not exist—there is only the bare valueless fact of existence" (1994, 61). On the atheistic side, Michael Ruse claims that "morality has no philosophically objective foundation" and "there are no foundations of any sort from which to derive morality—be these foundations evolution, God's will or whatever" (1995, 234). Ruse appears to assume that there are objective moral truths only if there is some nonmoral foundation from which such truths can be derived. I suggest that the plausibility of brute ethical facts suggests that such an assumption is implausible—or at least, stands in need of some sort of support.

The view that objective morality lacks an external foundation does not imply that particular instances of good and evil or rightness and wrongness have no source. In the next section I explain my view about the source of instances of good, evil, rightness, and wrongness.

Evil is directly robustly caused by certain natural features of the universe

Causing pain just for fun is a paradigmatic instance of an evil act. J. L. Mackie famously puzzled over the relationship between the natural property *causing pain just for fun* and the moral property *moral wrongness*:

> What is the connection between the natural fact that an action is a piece of deliberate cruelty—say, causing pain just for fun—and the moral fact that it is wrong? It cannot be an entailment, a logical or semantic necessity. Yet is it not merely that the two features occur together. The wrongness must somehow be "consequential" or "supervenient"; it is wrong because it is a piece of deliberate cruelty. But just *what in the world* is signified by this "because"? (1977, 41)

Given my view that *there being an objective normative reason to refrain from causing pain just for fun* (or, more simply, *being evil*) is a nonnatural property, Mackie's remarks suggest the following question for me: what is the relationship between the natural property *being an instance of causing pain just for fun* and the nonnatural property *being evil*? I think that a plausible answer to this question is that the relation in question is a causal one of a robust sort—the same sort of causal relation that, according to theists, holds between the properties of *being (strongly) willed by God* and *obtaining*. This causal relation does not depend on the existence of a law of nature connecting acts of divine will with states of affairs (indeed, theists typically hold that whatever laws of nature hold are themselves the products of divine willing). Theists typically maintain that if God (strongly) wills that p, this necessarily brings it about that p obtains. And there is no reason that acts of divine will cannot be simultaneous with their effects. Necessarily, if God wills at time t that p obtains at time t, then p obtains at time t. Furthermore, it has been argued that ordinary, non-theistic causation requires that "causes always occur simultaneously with their *immediate* effects" (Huemer and Kovitz 2003, 556). The relation between *being an instance of causing pain just for fun* and *being evil* shares all of those features: it does not depend on a law of nature connecting causing pain just for fun with being evil, being an instance of causing pain just for fun entails that an act is evil, and the two properties are possessed by the act simultaneously.

It may be helpful here to consider the doctrine of divine conservation. According to that doctrine, God not only brings all contingent things into existence but also sustains or keeps them in existence for each moment that they exist (see Kvanvig 2008 for a useful discussion of this doctrine). On at least some versions of this doctrine, there is a robust causal relation between divine willing and every contingent thing at each moment of its existence. One way of construing my proposal, then, is as a doctrine of *ethical conservation*: whatever ethical properties are instantiated are conserved or sustained by various underlying nonethical properties via a robust causal relation that holds between the relevant nonethical and ethical properties.

What, it might be asked, explains the presence of these robust causal connections in the universe? *Why* does the fact that an act is an instance of causing pain just for fun robustly cause that act to be evil rather than, say, good? Why does the fact that an act is an instance of causing pain just for fun robustly cause any ethical property to be instantiated at all? My answer is that nothing explains these robust causal connections. Such connections are part of the fundamental, bottom level of reality. It might be objected that such a view builds a suspiciously convenient (from a human perspective) degree of order and rationality into the basic structure of the universe. I agree that my view implies that, at a fundamental level, reality makes sense from a human point of view. But neither theistic nor non-theistic opponents of my view are well-positioned to argue that this is an objectionable feature of my view.

Theists are typically committed to the existence of the robust causal relation between God strongly willing that p and the obtaining of p. We might raise the following question for their view: *Why* does God strongly willing p robustly cause the obtaining of p rather than, say, not-p? Why does God strongly willing p robustly cause anything at all? It is hard to see what sort of explanation a theist can offer to these questions. At any rate, it is clear that the existence of such robust causal connections cannot be explained by appeal to divine acts of will, since the efficacy of such acts of will is the very thing that would need to be explained. It might be suggested that God's essential omnipotence explains the existence of these robust causal connections. But that proposal fails because the existence of the robust causal connection is itself a component of divine omnipotence. It appears, then, that my view and the theistic view both require the existence of robust causal connections that are rational and make sense (from a human perspective) and yet for which there is no explanation.

Atheists, for their part, typically hold that there are some basic laws of nature for which there is no deeper explanation (a commitment that theistic critics often argue is problematic). These basic laws of nature are suspiciously amenable to understanding by the human mind, often expressible as mathematical formulas; indeed, the contemporary physicist Brian Greene entertains the possibility that "reality is how math feels" (2011, 344). And so it seems that just about everyone is committed to the existence of some sort of fundamental, inexplicable rationality built into the basic structure of reality.

A related worry about the idea that there are robust causal connections between (instances of) nonmoral and moral properties is that we have no account of *how* such causation works. This worry is similar to the old worry often raised for substance dualists that we have no account of how causation between nonphysical souls and physical bodies could occur.[9] Commenting on this worry, contemporary Christian philosophers J. P. Moreland and William Lane Craig have this to say:

> A question about how A causally interacts with B is a request for an intervening mechanism between A and B that can be described. One can ask how turning the key starts a car because there is an intermediate electrical system between the key and the car's running engine that is the means by which turning the key causes the engine to start. . . . But the interaction between mind and body . . . most likely is . . . direct and immediate. There *is* no intervening mechanism, and thus a "how" question describing that mechanism does not even arise. (2003, 234–44)

I suggest that it is similarly plausible that there is no intervening mechanism that connects, for example, being an instance of causing pain just for fun with being an instance of evil; rather, the causal connection is direct and immediate.

If evil is directly robustly caused by certain instances of nonmoral properties, then one important element of the explanation of evil in the world is that the relevant nonmoral properties are instantiated. Because there is pain, there is evil; because there is cruelty, there is evil; and so on. A natural further question to ask is: why is there pain, intentional cruelty, and so on? It seems to me that these are empirical questions, the answers to which are provided by the relevant sciences. I think that evolutionary psychology has an important role to play in explaining the existence of much of the evil in our world. In the next section I examine the specific evil of dehumanization.

The evil of dehumanization

I understand *dehumanization* to be the denial of personhood or humanity to human persons. Dehumanization is a psychological phenomenon. If I dehumanize you, I do not literally take away your humanity; rather, I fail to recognize you as a human person despite the fact that you are one. An important consequence of dehumanization is that those who are dehumanized are seen as lacking the basic rights of human persons; because they are seen as nonhuman, they are seen as lacking human rights. Thus, dehumanization opens the door to all sorts of moral transgression against the dehumanized and there is much evidence that dehumanization is an essential ingredient in large-scale exploitation, enslavement, and genocide.

In his book-length treatment of dehumanization, David Livingstone Smith focuses on a particularly dangerous type of dehumanization in which the dehumanized are believed to be subhumans in human form. In these cases the dehumanized are not merely not seen as human; they are genuinely believed to be some type of noxious pest or animal in human form—typically a filthy pest, a predatory monster, or an animal of prey (Smith 2011, 251–62). Significantly, when people are viewed in this way they are not merely seen as lacking basic human rights; seeing people in such ways promotes the view that there is a moral imperative to wipe them out. A paradigmatic example of this phenomenon is the Nazi attitude toward Jews, who were seen as contagious pests that needed to be eradicated in order to protect Europe's moral purity

(Smith 2011, 154–62). Early in *Mein Kampf*, in Hitler's discussion of his transformation from a "soft-hearted cosmopolitan" to "an out-and-out anti-Semite" ([1939] 2011, 49), Hitler writes this:

> Was there any shady undertaking, any form of foulness . . . in which at least one Jew did not participate? On putting the probing knife carefully in that kind of abscess one immediately discovered, like a maggot in a putrescent body, a little Jew who was often blinded by the sudden light. ([1939] 2011, 45)

The discussion concludes with Hitler declaring: "In standing guard against the Jew I am defending the handiwork of the Lord" ([1939] 2011, 49). We see in these lines both the likening of Jews to nonhuman pests—indeed, Hitler describes Jews as "parasites" and "leeches" throughout *Mein Kampf*—and the assertion of a moral imperative to "stand against" such pests.

One of Smith's goals is to explicate the psychological mechanisms that make this sort of dehumanization possible. One such mechanism is what Smith calls "folk biology," an innate tendency to view living creatures as falling into categories (species) defined by fixed essences. Each such essence defines the true nature of each living being; it is causally responsible for the observable attributes of each living creature, yet the essence itself cannot be directly observed. According to folk biology, then, it is possible for a given creature to appear to be one type of being and yet in virtue of its underlying essence really be another type of being (Smith 2011, 186–96). Smith proposes that this folk biological thinking can be applied to human beings as well with the result that we are prone to dividing other people into different species on the basis of skin color, dress, and so on (Smith 2011, 197–98). The notion that a given creature is defined by its hidden inner essence makes it possible for us to believe that some beings that appear human on the outside are really some other type of creature in virtue of their hidden underlying essence (Smith 2011, 101).

This sort of application of folk biology to human beings is on display in *Mein Kampf*. In a chapter titled "Race and People," Hitler asserts that it is an "iron law of nature" that "each animal mates only with one of its own species" ([1939] 2011, 179). Hitler then appeals to this principle to try to derive certain conclusions about human beings. In doing so he engages in at least two confusions.

First, he moves from the descriptive claim that animals mate only with members of their own species to the moral claim that animals *ought* to mate only with members of their own species. Second, he mistakenly takes it that human beings of distinct races belong to distinct species, thereby misusing folk biology in just the way Smith describes. Indeed, toward the end of *Mein Kampf*, Hitler asserts that "we are members of the highest species of humanity on this earth" ([1939] 2011, 398). Combining these two confusions leads Hitler to the ridiculous conclusion that reproduction among members of different races results in "a progressive drying up of the vital sap" and "is a sin against the will of the Eternal Creator" ([1939] 2011, 180–81). Hitler also appeals to the sort of hidden essence described by Smith; for example, at one point he asserts that "the internal characteristics of a people are always the causes which determine the nature of the effect that outer circumstances have on them" ([1939] 2011, 182). Throughout *Mein Kampf* Hitler displays an obsession with preserving the purity of Aryan blood, an obsession that is based on his view that the quality of each "species" of human being is determined by the quality of its blood and that Aryan blood is of the highest quality. This is what we might characterize as a "blood-based" version of the idea that each creature's nature is determined by the nature of its hidden underlying essence.

The temptation to dehumanize arises when we are strongly motivated to exploit, enslave, or harm members of some other group. Dehumanization is a psychological trick that allows us to short-circuit our natural inhibitions against harming other human beings (Smith 2011, 250). Smith explains the results as follows:

> Demoting a population to subhuman status excludes them from the universe of moral obligation. Whatever responsibilities we have toward nonhuman animals, they are not the same as those we have toward members of our own species. So, if human-looking creatures are not really people, then we don't have to treat them as people. They can be used instrumentally, with complete disregard for their human worth—they can be killed, tortured, raped, experimented upon, and even eaten. (2011, 159)

James Waller explains that perpetrators' treatment of their victims can facilitate the dehumanization of those victims. If you treat people like animals, they will seem more like animals, and it will be psychologically easier to see them as nonhumans:

> Victims held as prisoners are often kept hungry and helpless. . . . They are often forced to scavenge through the garbage for food, steal food from others, or turn informant to receive food—all actions that result in dehumanization. Victims are also often forced to live in filth and urinate and defecate on themselves. They become emaciated figures of total misery, lice-infested, soiled, and wrapped in rags, furthering their dehumanization in the eyes of the perpetrators. (2007, 209)

Dehumanization is the source of, or at least a key ingredient in, the worst evils in human history. By freeing us from the restraints we would otherwise have against torturing, enslaving, and killing our fellow human beings, dehumanization unleashes the monster within us. Ironically, while the dehumanizer often believes her victim to be a subhuman monster, dehumanization makes the dehumanizer herself into a sort of monster.[10] Immanuel Kant proposed that the fundamental principle of morality is to "treat humanity . . . always at the same time as an end and never simply as a means" ([1785] 1993, 36). This is very close to: *don't dehumanize*. Dehumanization is a kind of evil that strikes at the very heart of morality.

Dehumanization also appears to be a uniquely human phenomenon that allows human beings to attain heights of cruelty and evil beyond the reach of any other animal.[11] As Mark Twain put it, "Man is the Cruel Animal" (quoted in Smith 2011, 203) and as the ancient Latin proverb has it, "Man is a wolf to man." Dehumanization, then, is grounded in human nature. Evolutionary forces have shaped our minds so that dehumanization comes easily to us, though the specific nature of dehumanization varies across cultures. As Smith puts it, dehumanization "has a form that cuts across cultures" but "its content in any given case is culturally determined" (2011, 265).

Traditional Christianity appeals to the Fall of Man to explain the evil that is now inherent in human nature. On this view, God did not create man as the Cruel Animal; rather, human nature was corrupted and spoiled through some sort of turning away from God, some original sin. As C. S. Lewis memorably puts it, through the Fall "a new species, never made by God, had sinned itself into existence" (1940, 79). Traditional Christians and contemporary atheists like myself agree that human nature is deeply flawed but we disagree about the explanation of that flawed nature, with Christians appealing to the Fall of Man and contemporary atheists appealing to our evolutionary origins.

Earlier I suggested that being an instance of causing pain just for fun robustly causes an act to be an instance of evil. The foregoing discussion of dehumanization suggests that dehumanization is an important contributing factor to many actual instances of causing pain just for fun. We see, then, how empirical science and philosophy might combine to yield an explanation for the existence of much of the evil in the world. Empirical science identifies dehumanization as a significant contributing factor to cruelty, enslavement, and genocide, and philosophical reflection suggests that *being evil* is a nonnatural property that is directly and robustly caused by properties like *being an instance of cruelty*, *being an instance of enslavement*, and *being an instance of genocide*.

Conclusion

What is the source of evil in a godless universe? I propose that objective morality has no foundation external to itself but instead ultimately rests on a foundation of basic ethical facts—necessary ethical truths with no external explanation. Some of these basic ethical facts are facts about evil—for example, that inflicting pain just for fun is evil. These basic ethical facts hold regardless of whether any ethical properties are actually instantiated. Let us suppose that in the early stages of the universe there was no life or consciousness; accordingly, goodness, evil, moral rightness, and wrongness were all uninstantiated. Through various natural processes life and eventually human beings arose; with human beings came the occurrence of inflicting suffering just for fun. The occurrence of such acts brought evil into the world by way of the robust causation I described earlier. In this way, evil is both objective and real in our godless universe.

Notes

1 See Parfit's discussion of good in the reason-implying sense (2011a, 38–39).

2 This distinction corresponds to my distinction between normative and psychological reasons (see Wielenberg 2005, 69), which I found in Blackburn (1998, 265); see also Crisp's distinction between normative and explanatory reasons (2006, 38).

3 Another example aimed at illustrating the possibility of agents having normative reasons of which they are unaware is Crisp's *Two Buttons* example (2006, 39).

4 This understanding of objectivity is similar to Shafer-Landau's (2003, 15) concept of stance-independence.

5 See, for example, Brink (1989, 166) and Adams (1999, 15–16).

6 It appears that legend is mistaken here and that Moore never gave any such argument; see Feldman (2005). However, for present purposes what matters is the nature of the legendary argument, not whether Moore ever gave it.

7 See also Enoch (2011, 104–08) and Bedke (2012).

8 This discussion of Chalmers's view and robust normative realism owes much to a blog post at PEA Soup by Jussi Suikkanen on November 19, 2010, titled "Chalmers and Naturalism," available online: http://peasoup.typepad.com/peasoup/2010/11/chalmers-and-naturalism.html (accessed January 12, 2018).

9 This objection seems to have originated with Princess Elisabeth of Bohemia in the seventeenth century. Elisabeth's statement of the objection can be found in her June 5, 1643 letter to Descartes, available online: http://www.earlymoderntexts.com/assets/pdfs/descartes1643_1.pdf (accessed January 12, 2018).

10 This theme is explored to powerful effect in the *Black Mirror* episode "Men against Fire."

11 Though there is evidence of a rudimentary version of the phenomenon in chimpanzees—"dechimpization." See de Waal (2005, 141) and Smith (2011, 204–14).

Response to Erik J. Wielenberg

Richard Brian Davis

Erik J. Wielenberg's rich and nuanced chapter offers an explanation of evil, building on his previous work in metaethics—a view he calls *robust normative realism* ((128) hereafter, RNR).[1] According to RNR, evil is a normative, nonphysical property that can be exemplified by "states of affairs, actions, intentions, and persons" (123). Although it is an objective feature of our universe, *being evil* is neither a natural property (e.g., *being painful*) nor a supernatural property (e.g., *being prohibited by God*). Evil exists because it stands in a "robust causal relation" to certain "underlying non-ethical properties" (132).

In addition to what he takes to be RNR's internal virtues, Wielenberg also cites an external theoretical advantage: RNR's consistency with naturalism. Like Ruse, he endorses the causal closure of the physical but with a *caveat*:

> I endorse the existence of non-physical properties but do not reject the causal closure of the physical or deny that the physical sciences are entirely successful in their own domains. If naturalistic dualists [like David Chalmers] can get by without invoking the forces of darkness, then so can robust normative realists. (128)

The overall position, then, is RNR *plus*: the conjunction of RNR (with its nonnatural properties) and naturalism (N)—defined sparsely as the view that (quoting Chalmers) "everything is a consequence of a network of basic [physical] properties and laws" (ibid.). And since Wielenberg holds both RNR and N, he is of course thinking of them as perfectly compatible.

Here it is helpful to note that these two theses are distinct. RNR neither entails (nor is it entailed by) N. So while RNR&N is obviously incompatible with theism, it is by no means clear that

RNR is. Indeed, something very like RNR was defended by the Christian philosopher Samuel Clarke (1675–1729) in his Boyle Lectures of 1705.[2] So the "Godless Normative Realism" Wielenberg refers to in the subtitle of *Robust Ethics* is almost certainly derived from N alone. There is nothing in RNR, so far as I can see, that need trouble a Christian theist.

In what follows, I want to raise a couple of concerns about RNR, and then surface a slightly deeper worry about the compatibility of RNR and N. But let's start with what Wielenberg says about evil. He proposes that something is evil just if there is "a reason to avoid or eliminate the thing" (123). This isn't all there is to evil, but "it is one important element," in which case "evil has a normative component" (ibid.). And since on his view normative reasons are objective, we can say that (on RNR) the property of being evil (E) includes the property of there being an objective normative reason to avoid such-and-such (A). The fact that E includes A is then used to show ("from the armchair" (127) as it were) that E can't be identified with either a natural property (NP) or a supernatural property (SP):

> There being an objective normative reason to avoid or eliminate such-and-such is of a fundamentally different type than any natural or supernatural property and hence being evil is neither a natural nor a supernatural property. (ibid.)

So the idea is that you can't turn E into an NP or an SP, since it includes A—a "fundamentally different type" of property from either. The assumption here seems to be that, for example, A and SP properties are incompatible. But *whether* they are, I think, is surely going to depend on how we frame the relevant properties. Consider the evil of *depriving myself of the use of reason*—however you look at it, an evil for any philosopher. If you're a theist, you might think this evil includes the following A property:

A*: Having been commanded by God to avoid "great intemperance and ungoverned passions"[3] lest I deprive myself of the use of reason.

Now A* is arguably objective. It also constitutes a normative reason to avoid depriving myself of my reason, since it "count(s) in favor of [my] having some attitude, or acting in some way" (124).[4]

Still further, it is almost certainly a supernatural property, since it involves God's having commanded something. So here we have an A property that isn't of a "fundamentally different type" than an SP property. In fact, it *is* an SP property. So there is no incompatibility between A and SP properties at all.

Another feature of RNR is its commitment to basic ethical facts. These are necessarily obtaining states of affairs, involving ethical properties like *being evil*. Following Plantinga, Wielenberg takes states of affairs to be "necessarily existing abstract entities" (128). The important thing to note about basic ethical facts is they are *brute facts*: their "obtaining is not explained by the obtaining of other states of affairs" (129). Like the state of affairs *7 and 5's equaling 12*, there is "no external explanation" (138) for why they are actual. They simply are. Thus Wielenberg says,

> To ask of such facts, "Where do they come from?" or "On what foundation do they rest?" is misguided in much the way that, according to many theists, it is misguided to ask of God, "Where does He come from?" or "On what foundation does He rest?" (130)

Now I certainly agree that there are states of affairs, that some of them involve ethical properties, and that some of these obtain necessarily. It's less clear to me that the obtaining of basic ethical facts requires "no external explanation." For one thing, if we're following Plantinga, a fact is still an abstract state of affairs. To be sure, nothing explains the *existence* of a fact; it exists by a necessity of its own nature. It doesn't follow that nothing explains its *being actual* or *obtaining*.

Consider the RNR explanation of evil in the world. It proceeds by way of an example. The nonnatural property

E: Being evil

is "directly robustly caused," (138)[5] we are told, by the natural property

F: Being an instance of causing pain for the fun of it.

The connection here is brute. There is "no intervening mechanism" or explanation for why it obtains. Rather, "the causal connection is direct and immediate" (133). Let's say that's right. What that means is that *E's being caused by F* is a necessary state of affairs—an uninstantiated abstract object at best. It's not a fact, however, until it is *made actual* by something—something external to the state of affairs itself. Wielenberg himself seems to recognize this when he notes that "one important element of the explanation of evil in the world is that the relevant non-moral properties are *instantiated*" (134; emphasis added).

I think Wielenberg is correct here. Thinking just of the case at hand, given the necessary one-way causal connection between E and F, E will be instantiated only if *F's causing E* obtains or is actual. But that will be the case only if F is instantiated. There has to be a trope or property instance of F. What we require, in other words, is the very thing Wielenberg says we don't need: an external explanation or actuality-maker. And this takes us to the heart of the matter, but also I fear the heart of the difficulties. Just how is a nonmoral property like F to be instantiated? *Who* instantiates it? If no one can or does, then *being evil* simply won't be instantiated; evil won't exist.

If we think about F carefully, I think we can see that only a conscious rational agent with the power of choice could bring it about that F is instantiated in such a way that the evil that was thereby brought into the world was something for which she was responsible. Here the explanatory resources of RNR wind up, and Wielenberg must at last find an ally in Ruse:

> Let us suppose that in the early stages of the universe there was no life or consciousness; accordingly, goodness, evil, moral rightness and wrongness were all uninstantiated. Through various natural processes life and eventually human beings arose; with human beings came the occurrence of inflicting suffering just for fun. The occurrence of such acts brought evil into the world by way of the robust causation I described earlier. In this way, evil is both objective and real in our godless universe. (138)

Let's suppose that I've supposed that originally there was no God, but somehow there was a universe. (That's a rather big ask, but okay.) And then in that universe—naturally enough, since there was no God—"there was no life or consciousness." That seems right.

What should I expect from that point? Consciousness, agency, rationality, and choice? I don't see it. I'm afraid I'm with Clarke on this:[6]

> If there ever was a time when there was nothing in the universe but matter and motion, there never could have been anything else therein but matter and motion. And it would have been as impossible there should ever have existed any such thing as intelligence, or consciousness . . . as it is now impossible for motion to be blue or red, or for a triangle to be transformed into a sound. (1705 [1998], 42)

And then it would have been just as impossible that there should ever have been evil. But there is.

Paul Helm

In this rejoinder to Wielenberg, I shall devote most of the space to the comparisons he draws between his metaethic and theological, or what he prefers to call, supernatural ethics. His willingness to make thoughtful cross-comparisons like this is an attractive part of his style, or of his temperament. But before I do that I should like to comment on another feature of his procedure.

He tells us that evil is multifarious and that "among the kinds of things that can be evil are states of affairs, actions, intentions, and persons" (123). But in his examples of evil in fact only two stand out: maltreating someone just for fun, and variants of that; and Augustine's example of his theft of pears, and variants of that. These are convincing examples for his readers in that most civilized people would nod in agreement. We are not as other men are. The first looks like a case of sadism, the second a case of gratuitous theft. There are normative reasons to refrain from performing these actions, and they are objectively evil.

Examples are significant in philosophy. I wonder why these were chosen but hazard that it is because they are cases of evil actions or states of affairs that are indisputably evil, that is, in the polite circles of analytic philosophers, if not in those of sadists, or of "mindless youngsters."

Cases that are disputable would not serve Wielenberg's cause. But he is proposing a metaethic, and it's a fundamental attitude to ethics that the central examples are essentially contestable. But faced with examples that are uniformly, or for the most part, not contestable it is more convincing to be persuaded that normative reasons, as Wielenberg says, are "out there in the world" (125). Put in another way, what makes his nonnaturalism even remotely plausible is that it rests on the slenderest set of cases. If one were to expand the set to take in the many contestable examples that we meet, then the examples of evil would increase, but by adding contestable cases, his objectivist metaethic does not look so secure.

This highlights the need for some epistemology, about which he says little or nothing. If we agree about the sadism this is likely to be (for the nonnaturalist) that our moral antennae, intuitions, or moral senses, are giving the same reading, well and good. But what are we to say when there is discord, and on a large scale, as there is in our pluralist societies? What if a person's entire identity is bound up with certain views? Appeals to moral intuition then flounder, and nonnaturalism becomes much less plausible. It is a pity that Wielenberg did not say something on this side of things.

There is a similar unsatisfactoriness, for a similar reason, about his statement,

> But what is it for something to be evil? Part of the answer to that question, I believe, is that for something to be evil is for there to be a reason to avoid or eliminate the thing. I do not claim that this is all there is to being evil, but it is one important element of evil. (123)

But the point is that for many actions or states of affairs, there are social disagreements about whether that action ought to be avoided or eliminated. Think of the different ideas there are (and have been) about bringing up children.

Another thing that caught my eye is an argument of Wielenberg's for the objective-subjective distinction. For example, he says "funniness is subjective, because whether a joke is funny depends on whether people would be amused by it" (125). He notes that happiness is objective in his sense because "whether a person is happy depends on the attitude of someone—namely, the person himself—but it does not depend upon the attitudes of *observers towards* him" (125). These general claims, endorsed by Wielenberg, strike me as plainly false. Some people may, and others may not, be amused by the joke. What then? And I may be the sort of person whose happiness is a kind of reflective state *consisting in* the reactions of "observers" who have certain attitudes to me.

So at certain points the bricks out of which Wielenberg builds his edifice do not appear to be able to bear the strain that is placed on them. I come now to the comparisons he draws with aspects of theology.

An aspect of Wielenberg's ethical nonnaturalism is that it has about it a certain kind of bruteness. On this view, the nonnatural views—normative reasons are "out there in the world" (ibid.). He suggests that there are interesting parallels and divergencies (just as interesting) between such an ethical view and theism. But from the fact that the existence of God is brute—or can be held to be—it does not follow that what God wills is similarly brute. We might distinguish here between bruteness of God's existence and that of his will. His existence, being necessary, cannot be other than brute, but what he wills, may be brute only for a time. This is relevant to the explanation of the incidence of evil. Further, a theist may hold that the obligatoriness of an action may consist in God's revealed will, his commands, but puzzle about certain states of affairs that are so commanded. Surely one could think of factors that make sadism an evil—for example, the dissonance between deliberately causing pain or the enjoyment of it or the trivializing of it, as "for fun." Suppose the pain is inflicted by consent, in a research program, say, then the evil lessens, as it does were the person quickly to get used to the pain.

Wielenberg asks,

> What is the relationship between the natural property *being an instance of causing pain just for fun* and the non-natural property *being evil*? I think that a plausible answer to this question is that the relation in question is a causal one of a robust sort— the same sort of causal relation that, according to theists, holds between the properties of *being (strongly) willed by God* and *obtaining*. (131)

It is necessitating, but causal, and so not causal in the everyday sense. The problem in appealing to the theological example is that this is a case of divine action, intentionally willed, and so on. But there is something amusing in a secularist like Wielenberg (and one like J. L. Mackie too) receiving relief from an appeal to something that has the character of extramundane agency. In actual fact Wielenberg comes to the view that this is a case of conceptual causation (132). These "robust" causal relations, as Wielenberg calls them, are not explicable by anything or anyone. They are simply there. At this point the elevator reaches the ground floor in its downward trajectory.

However, the theist is in no better place, Wielenberg avers.

> We might raise the following question for their view: *why* does God strongly willing *p* robustly cause the obtaining of *p* rather than, say, not-*p*? Why does God strongly willing *p* robustly cause anything at all? It is hard to see what sort of explanation a theist can offer to these questions. At any rate, it is clear that the existence of such robust causal connections cannot be explained by appeal to divine acts of will, since the efficacy of such acts of will is the very thing that would need to be explained. (ibid.)

He may have partly, if not wholly, provided the explanation by asserting that "if God (strongly) wills that *p*, this necessarily brings it about that *p* obtains" (131). Is it the efficacy of such acts that need explaining, or the choices of such acts? As he explains, all cases of God strongly willing have this robust character, due to his role as Creator and Lord of humankind. But I don't see that this follows, except that human beings have a complex nature, being able to disobey, and to do so for a trivial pleasure. But there is of course the general question of why God wills anything that he does will. As to the question of why people are sadistic, this may be an empirical question in explaining which the old, old story of evolutionary psychology has an important role to play.

With so much that he cannot explain about his ethical nonnaturalism, it is interesting to have Wielenberg's treatment of the specific evil of dehumanization (134). This is an admirable part of his essay. He sees dehumanization as a source of humans' causing people pain just for fun. He claims, "Traditional Christians and contemporary atheists like myself agree that human nature is deeply flawed but we disagree about the explanation of that flawed nature" (138). I agree, though this is a small beginning.

Michael Ruse

True confession time. I am not an analytic philosopher. I am best described as being in the tradition of Arthur Lovejoy and Isaiah Berlin, a historian of ideas who uses the history to approach philosophical ideas. Which is no doubt fine and dandy, but it does mean that I am at somewhat of a disadvantage when I encounter a full-blown analytic philosopher like Erik J. Wielenberg. I simply cannot understand what they are saying. I say this in shame not pride.

I am part of a group project, so I cannot back out now. Do understand that I may be badly off the mark. Actually, the place where I do feel most comfortable with Wielenberg's piece is with his final paragraph. Let me quote it in full because I will use this as my take-off point.

> What is the source of evil in a godless universe? I propose that objective morality has no foundation external to itself but instead ultimately rests on a foundation of basic ethical facts—necessary ethical truths with no external explanation. Some of these basic ethical facts are facts about evil—for example, that inflicting pain just for fun is evil. These basic ethical facts hold regardless of whether any ethical properties are actually instantiated. Let us suppose that in the early stages of the universe there was no life or consciousness; accordingly, goodness, evil, moral rightness and wrongness were all uninstantiated. Through various natural processes life and eventually human beings arose; with human beings came the occurrence of inflicting suffering just for fun. The occurrence of such acts brought evil into the world by way of the robust causation I described earlier. In this way, evil is both objective and real in our godless universe. (138)

I can understand this and more importantly disagree with it!

My position is that evil is all part of evolved human nature. No humans, no evil. For me, questions like "Does the tree make a sound in the forest when it falls, if there is no one around to hear it?" don't make any sense. If there were no humans ever, judging the moral status of the Holocaust doesn't make sense to me. If you say to me, "Ah, but think if humans did exist, what then?" unhesitatingly I would say that the Holocaust was evil. That is because humans have been put in the picture. This is obviously where Wielenberg and I disagree completely. He thinks, humans or not—humans or not even conceived of (perhaps not even conceivable)—the Holocaust was evil.

As I see it, as a nonbeliever, Wielenberg now has three options. He can go for a naturalistic account where evil is somehow inherent in the nature of natural things. Or he can go for a nonnaturalistic account which seems to offer two options. Either you say that evil exists (presumably necessarily) in some nonnatural world (one suspects mathematical truths are also going to be part of this world) or you say that evil doesn't exist outside humans but it has a necessity that my position obviously lacks. You could still call the Holocaust evil even if humans never had or could exist.

The naturalistic position sees value in nature and goes from there. The Holocaust was natural, in the metaphysical sense, and deeply nonnatural in the ethical sense. It is a view that was favored by Herbert Spencer (1879) in the nineteenth century and more recently in the last and present centuries by the biologist Edward O. Wilson (Wilson 1975). Today's most vocal philosophical defender is Robert J. Richards (Richards 1986; Ruse and Richards 2017) of the University of Chicago. The position ignores (or discounts) the is-ought distinction. This has long for me been the stumbling block. Now I am not quite so sure. A year or two back I spent time in Stellenbosch in the wine-growing area of South Africa. It is the most beautiful place in the world. If some mining company came alone and proposed cutting off the top of one of the adjacent mountains, I would be the first to cry "rape," and if that isn't finding value in physical things, I don't know what is. I also a year or two back wrote a book on the Gaia hypothesis and that too set me thinking (Ruse 2013).

Wielenberg goes with G. E. Moore on this, as I do more or less. For the purposes of this piece, move on. If only because of the reference to Moore, who thought of his thinking on nonnatural properties as following Plato—"I am pleased to believe that this is the most Platonic system of modern times" (Baldwin 1990, 50)—I did expect to find some nod at the Greek philosopher. I was disappointed so— showing why I disagree with Wielenberg's conclusion—let me fill in some details. I take it that you believe in some other dimension of existence in which there are eternal truths. In one sense, I am not about to deny this. I am not sure I could. In fact, living in this weird world of ours with things like consciousness and quantum entanglement, I endorse the sentiments of fellow nonbeliever J. B. S. Haldane. "I have no doubt that in reality the future will be vastly more surprising than anything I can imagine. . . . Now my own suspicion is that the Universe is not only queerer than we suppose, but queerer than we *can* suppose" (Haldane 1927, 310; 286).

My problem is how we humans in this world are to get in touch with that world. As a nonbeliever, you cannot simply say: "Well we have had lots of experience of contacting the other world, namely the world of God. So why not suppose a bit more ontology, which might in fact be part of that other world we know already?" You have to say something like: "We have (natural) intuitions into this other world. 2 + 2 = 4 really is true. So why not morality? The Holocaust was evil. Go from there." To which I am going to reply that I want to know a lot more about this supposedly natural power of intuition, and why I should not simply accept my own position— these beliefs were put into place by natural selection because it was adaptively advantageous to have them, and the same goes for the sense of objectivity, about which we are talking now.

Another objection you might have is that the world of morality— in the tradition of the Platonic Forms—could never house evil. Plato excluded "undignified" things like hair, mud, and dirt. I am not sure that you are caught though. You simply play the Christian trick of denying true existence to evil—God could never have created it— and defining it against the good. Just as you don't have a Form of 2 + 2 = 5, but define it against the Form of 2 + 2 = 4. The Holocaust is evil because of the absence of good. I confess that I myself am not entirely happy with this. I want the evil of Heinrich Himmler to equal the good of Sophie Scholl, at the metaphysical level that is. Of course, I don't have the problem of everything having been created by a good god.

The other position, which finds necessity without God, is that which argues that it is all a matter of the conditions of proper or rational thinking. This is the Kantian position, one that I tried to show (in my piece) I much respect even if in the end I reject it. Again, I am not sure on Wielenberg's stance. The one reference to Kant is to this philosopher's views more at the substantive than the metaethical level of discussion. It is a favorable nod to Kant's claim that we should treat people as ends and not as means. You will see that I have myself endorsed this, so clearly that is not quite where we are having disagreements. If it is a question of the metaethics, the necessity, then you know where I stand. Whatever the status of mathematics, I do think it is involved here in the guise of game theory. I am quite prepared to accept that any kind of moral interaction has to follow some rules—I would say that otherwise you get selected out of the game, quickly—and I am even prepared to say that evil acts may well fall afoul of the best optimizing strategy. However, I am not sure we have morality. As I point out, in the end Kant wasn't really either.

Whatever the reasons, this I can say: Wielenberg and I are on different sides.

Notes

1 See also, Wielenberg (2014, 14).

2 Clarke gave the Boyle Lectures in consecutive years in 1704–05. The second of these lectures was published as *A Discourse Concerning the Unchangeable Obligations of Natural Religion and the Truth and Certainty of the Christian Revelation* (Clarke 1708).

3 Clarke (1708, 191).

4 The quote is from Derek Parfit (2011a, 31).

5 In some places the relation is said to be that of entailment. Compare "being an instance of causing pain just for fun *entails* that an act is evil" (132, emphasis added).

6 For some (but by no means all) of the details, see my lead essay in Chapter 1 of this volume.

Reply to Critics

Erik J. Wielenberg

I'm grateful to my fellow contributors for their careful attention to my initial essay. I think it will be most sensible to divide the various concerns they raise into metaphysical concerns and epistemological concerns and address them thematically rather than responding to each contributor in turn. But I first want to endorse Davis's suggestion that there is nothing in my metaethical theory itself (what he labels "RNR") that is at odds with Christian theism. My aim in developing RNR was to develop a plausible theory of objective morality that entails that there are objective ethical facts even if God does not exist, but RNR itself is not intended to rule out the truth of Christian theism. Of course, my own view is atheistic, but the metaethical component of my view is intended to be compatible with both theism and atheism. I turn now to some (but not all) of the challenges to my view raised by Davis, Helm, and Ruse.

Metaphysical concerns

Davis questions my view that moral properties like *being evil* are distinct from supernatural properties. Davis considers this property: *having been commanded by God to avoid great intemperance and ungoverned passions* (A*). Davis proposes that A* "constitutes a normative reason to avoid depriving myself of my reason" and hence A* is a property that is both normative and supernatural (141). The key word here is "constitutes." Does A* "constitute" a reason to avoid reason-deprivation in the sense that (a) instantiating A* *entails* or *robustly causes* someone to have a reason to avoid reason-deprivation or (b) to have a reason to avoid reason-deprivation *just is* to instantiate A*? My view is that (a) is plausible but (b) is not. One way of supporting such a position involves an appeal to a version of Parfit's Triviality Objection (2011b, 343). Suppose for the sake of argument that (b) is true. If (b) is true, then A* and *having a reason to avoid reason-deprivation* are the very same property. Given that assumption, the claim that (G) *if God has commanded you to avoid depriving yourself of reason, then you have a reason to avoid depriving yourself of reason* is not a substantive normative claim in that it isn't a claim with which someone might reasonably disagree or a claim that tells us something we didn't already know. Yet (G) seems to be substantive in that way, which suggests that (b) is false—though (a), of course, may still be true. So I am skeptical that moral properties can be fully reduced to supernatural (or natural, for that matter) properties.

Helm wonders about the adequacy of my suggestion that the relationship between the natural property *being an instance of causing pain just for fun* and the nonnatural property *being evil* is a robustly causal relation that itself has no further explanation. As Helm notes, with this robust causal relation, the explanatory "elevator reaches the ground floor" (147). In my initial essay, I drew parallels between the relation between the natural and nonnatural properties mentioned above and the relation between God's (strongly) willing that *p* and the obtaining of *p*. But it also seems to me that at least many Christian theists—those who adhere to Anselmian or perfect being theology—share even more similar ground with adherents of my view. In particular, adherents of my RNR and adherents of perfect being theology face similar puzzles. The key here is the Anselmian theist's commitment to the view that certain properties are *great-making properties*[1] that necessarily *make* things that have them great.[2] Examples include power and knowledge. God allegedly possesses great-making properties to the maximum degree; that's what *makes* Him unsurpassably great. It seems to me that whatever puzzles a proponent of a view like mine faces in accounting for the relationship between, say, being an instance of causing pain just for fun and being morally wrong, is matched by corresponding puzzles about the relationship between being powerful and being great. In the case of the former relationship, I posit a robust causal connection. Even if the Anselmian theist rejects this option in the case of the relation between divine power and divine greatness, the theist must think that there is *some* acceptable solution to this puzzle, which makes it hard to see how the theist can at the same time deny that there is an acceptable solution to the corresponding puzzle for the RNR-er.

Finally, Davis argues that, even granting the truth of the metaethical aspect of my overall worldview, because my view implies that there was a time when the universe was devoid of "consciousness, agency, rationality, and choice" (144), if my view were true then all of those things—and hence evil as well—would not exist. As I think Davis would agree, that claim depends on the sort of argument that he gave in his lead chapter. In my reply to that chapter, I sought to raise doubts about Davis's argument by drawing on the O'Connor-inspired view that I labeled *Naturalistic Emergentism*.

Epistemological concerns

Helm and Ruse both raise epistemological worries about my view, though their worries are slightly different. Helm's worry seems to be grounded in the existence of significant moral disagreement or variation in moral belief—not just across cultures but within them. Helm writes, "What are we to say when there is discord, and on a large scale, as there is in our pluralist societies? . . . Appeals to moral intuition then flounder, and non-naturalism becomes much less plausible" (145). Ruse, too, wants more information about how human beings might obtain knowledge of nonnatural moral features of reality, though his challenge focuses not on moral disagreement but rather on the alleged evolutionary origins of our moral beliefs:

> You have to say something like: "We have (natural) intuitions into this other world. 2+2=4 really is true. So why not morality? The Holocaust was evil. Go from there." To which I am going to reply that I want a lot more about this supposedly natural power of intuition, and why I should not simply accept my own position—these beliefs were put into place by natural selection because it was adaptively advantageous to have them, and the same goes for the sense of objectivity. (150)

These requests for more information about the epistemological side of things are certainly fair, and two of the four chapters of my recent book *Robust Ethics* are devoted to epistemological issues. My moral epistemology has some complexity to it and I will not be able to do it full justice here, but I will attempt to provide at least a sketch.[3] Let's begin with some recent work in empirical moral psychology.

Psychologists have come to recognize the importance of "mental processes that are inaccessible to consciousness but that influence judgments, feelings, or behavior"—what Timothy Wilson calls "the adaptive unconscious" (2002, 23). The operations of the adaptive unconscious are fast, automatic, and effortless, whereas the operations of the conscious mind are slow and effortful (Wilson 2002, 49). The cognitive system responsible for the former sort of cognition has come to be known as "System 1" and the cognitive system responsible for the latter sort of cognition has come to be known as "System 2" (Kahneman 2011, 19–105). Daniel Kahneman notes that System 1 "operates automatically and quickly, with little or no effort and no sense of voluntary control" whereas System 2 "allocates attention to the effortful mental activities that demand it . . . [its] operations . . . are often associated with the subjective experience of agency, choice, and concentration" (2011, 20–21). Much recent work in moral psychology suggests that System 1 cognition has a large (though not exclusive) role to play in generating our moral judgments. Behind what philosophers often call "moral intuition" is some complicated cognitive machinery operating largely outside of conscious awareness.

Kahneman suggests that the phenomenon of forming beliefs by way of cognitive processes to which we lack direct conscious access—which he calls "knowing without knowing how"—is quite common. It is thus plausible that System 1 cognition can produce justified beliefs and knowledge. An externalist approach to justification can accommodate such a view. Consider a simple version of *reliabilism* according to which a belief is justified just in case it is produced by a cognitive process that is reliable in the sense that it tends to generate more true beliefs than false ones. On this view, System 1 cognition can justify beliefs so long as the relevant cognitive processes tend to get things right; whether the believer has direct conscious access to the underlying processes or inputs is irrelevant.

Some theorists emphasize the parallels between grammatical knowledge and moral knowledge (see Horgan and Timmons 2007, 287–88, and Mikhail 2011). While there is much debate about such alleged parallels, one shared element is the presence of *dumbfounding*. Competent speakers of a language can often "just see" whether various sentences in that language are grammatically correct or incorrect but struggle when it comes to identifying a plausible grammatical principle that justifies their specific grammatical judgments. Similarly, in the moral domain, people often find themselves confidently making moral judgments for which they can provide no adequate foundation; trolley cases are a rich source of this moral dumbfounding.

Accordingly, there is wide agreement among contemporary moral psychologists about the following principle:

THE HIDDEN PRINCIPLES CLAIM: Our conscious moral judgments typically conform to general moral principles; such principles are *often but not always hidden* from us in that we cannot become consciously aware of the conformance of our conscious moral judgments to such principles in any direct way. This phenomenon is a consequence of the heavy involvement of System 1 cognition in the production of our conscious moral judgments.

Suppose I look around my office and have the visual experience of a yellow notebook resting on my desk. I form the belief that there is a yellow notebook on my desk. But it's not the case that I consciously reason this way: "I have the visual experience of a yellow notebook; therefore, there probably is a yellow notebook in front of me." Instead, when my perceptual faculties are functioning normally, the visual experience automatically triggers the belief about the notebook. Assuming that I have no defeaters for my belief that there is a yellow notebook on my desk, that belief constitutes knowledge.

Now consider Gilbert Harman's famous example: "You round a corner and see a group of young hoodlums pour gasoline on a cat and ignite it" (1977, 4). Harman suggests that in this case "you do not need to *conclude* that what they are doing is wrong; you do not need to figure anything out; you can *see* that it is wrong" (1977, 4). There are various plausible ways of fleshing out this simple example that are compatible with the Hidden Principles Claim. Here is one: you round the corner and perceive the hoodlums and their actions. Your brain produces various nonconscious classifications of the perceived act; in this case, let us suppose that one of these classifications is *torturing a cat just for fun.* This classification is produced by System 1; you do not consciously form the belief: "Those hoodlums are torturing a cat just for fun!" This classification triggers feelings of disgust and outrage in you, and those feelings in turn produce the conscious belief that what the hoodlums are doing is evil. Just as there is a smooth, automatic transition from having the visual experience of a notebook to believing that the notebook is on the desk, in the moral case there is a smooth, automatic transition from perceiving the hoodlums' actions to nonconsciously classifying the act as a case of cat-torture-for-fun to forming the conscious belief that their actions are evil—a transition that is accomplished by a flurry of behind-the-scenes System 1 activity.

On my view, instances of moral and nonmoral properties are interwoven together and robust causation is the cement that binds instances of these properties to each other. Although instances of moral properties themselves are causally inert, the nonmoral properties that generate them are not. When the nonmoral properties our System 1 cognition attends to in nonconsciously classifying things are reliably correlated with moral properties, moral beliefs can be epistemically justified.

I take it that evolutionary processes have instilled certain moral principles into most human beings—a possible example being the Doctrine of Double Effect discussed in my initial essay—but that culture and upbringing tweak these principles, which contributes to the moral pluralism pointed out by Helm. As Aristotle observes,

> As regards men, there is considerable variation. The same things give delight to some and pain to others, are painful and hateful to some and pleasant and agreeable to others. We find this also true of sweetness: the same things do not seem sweet to a man in fever and to a healthy person. Nor is the same thing hot to an invalid and to a man in good condition. (1999, 1176a10–15)

In the case of pleasure, Aristotle says that "what seem [to a virtuous person] to be pleasures are pleasures and what he enjoys is pleasant" (1999, 1176a15–20). Aristotle's view is that when one's emotional dispositions have been properly calibrated with moral reality, then anger, pleasure, and the like will be reliable indicators of moral truth. Whether that is the case depends heavily upon one's upbringing and cultural background. When it comes to whether our moral cognition generates knowledge, upbringing "makes a considerable difference, or, rather, all the difference" (1999, 1103b20–25).

While I am painfully aware of the incompleteness of this sketch, my hope is that it will provide the reader with some sense of the epistemological side of my view and of how we might acquire knowledge of evil in a godless universe.

Notes

1   For a discussion of great-making properties by a prominent Anselmian, see Plantinga (1974b, 199–200).

2   More precisely, having such properties makes things greater than they would otherwise be, everything else being equal. I ignore this subtlety in the main text to save words.

3   The rest of this section draws heavily from (Wielenberg 2014, chapter 3).

RECOMMENDED READING

The following recommended reading list has been subdivided into four general categories that cover many of the substantive issues touched on in this book. Those categories are: evil (as a general concept), the problem of evil, free will, and ethics. For those who are interested in pursuing those issues in more detail, hopefully this list will serve as a useful starting point.

Evil

Arendt, Hannah. (1963). *Eichmann in Jerusalem: A Report on the Banality of Evil*. New York: Penguin.

Calder, Todd. (2016). "The Concept of Evil." *The Stanford Encyclopedia of Philosophy* (Winter 2016 Edition), ed. Edward N. Zalta. Available online https://plato.stanford.edu/archives/win2016/entries/concept-evil/ (accessed June 7, 2018).

Card, Claudia. (2002). *The Atrocity Paradigm: A Theory of Evil*. Oxford: Oxford University Press.

Card, Claudia. (2010). *Confronting Evils: Torture, Terrorism and Genocide*. Cambridge, UK: Cambridge University Press.

Cole, Phillip. *The Myth of Evil: Demonizing the Enemy*. Westport, CT: Praeger, 2006.

Kant, Immanuel. ([1793] 1960). *Religion Within the Limits of Reason Alone*, trans. Theodore M. Green and John R. Silber. La Salle, IL: Open Court Publishing.

Kekes, John. (2005). *The Roots of Evil*. Ithaca: Cornell University Press.

Morton, Adam. (2004). *On Evil*. New York: Routledge.

McGinn, Colin. (1997). *Ethics, Evil, and Fiction*. Oxford: Clarendon.

Russell, Luke. (2014). *Evil: A Philosophical Investigation*. Oxford: Oxford University Press.

The Problem of Evil

Adams, Marilyn. (1999). *Horrendous Evils and the Goodness of God.* Ithaca: Cornell University Press.

Adams, Marilyn, and Robert Adams, eds. (1991). *The Problem of Evil.* Oxford: Oxford University Press.

Hick, John. (1977). *Evil and the God of Love,* 2nd ed. New York: Palgrave Macmillan.

Howard-Snyder, Daniel, ed. (1996). *The Evidential Argument from Evil.* Bloomington: Indiana University Press.

Mackie, J. L. (1982). *The Miracle of Theism: Arguments For and Against the Existence of God.* Oxford: Clarendon.

McBrayer, Justin, and Daniel Howard-Snyder, eds. (2013). *Blackwell Companion to the Problem of Evil.* Malden, MA: John Wiley & Sons, Inc.

Meister, Chad, and Paul Moser. (2017). *The Cambridge Companion to the Problem of Evil.* New York: Cambridge University Press.

Plantinga, Alvin. (1974). *The Nature of Necessity.* Oxford: Clarendon.

Rowe, William. (2001). *God and the Problem of Evil.* Oxford: Wiley-Blackwell.

Stump, Eleonore. (2010). *Wandering in Darkness: Narrative and the Problem of Suffering.* Oxford: Oxford University Press.

Swinburne, Richard. (1998). *Providence and the Problem of Evil.* Oxford: Oxford University Press.

van Inwagen, Peter. (2006). *The Problem of Evil.* Oxford: Oxford University Press.

Free Will

Clarke, Randolph. (2003). *Libertarian Accounts of Free Will.* New York: Oxford University Press.

Dennett, Daniel C. (1984). *Elbow Room: The Varieties of Free Will Worth Wanting.* Cambridge, MA: MIT Press.

Kane, Robert. (2005). *A Contemporary Introduction to Free Will.* New York: Oxford University Press.

Kane, Robert, ed. (2005). *The Oxford Handbook of Free Will.* Oxford: Oxford University Press.

Fischer, John Martin, and Mark Ravizza. (1998). *Responsibility and Control: A Theory of Moral Responsibility.* Cambridge, UK: Cambridge University Press.

Fischer, John Martin, Robert Kane, Derk Pereboom, and Manuel Vargas. (2007). *Four Views on Free Will. Great Debates in Philosophy.* Malden, MA: Blackwell.

O'Connor, Timothy. (2000). *Persons and Causes: The Metaphysics of Free Will.* Oxford: Oxford University Press.

O'Connor, Timothy. (2016). "Free Will." *The Stanford Encyclopedia of Philosophy* (Summer 2016 Edition), ed. Edward N. Zalta. Available online https://plato.stanford.edu/archives/sum2016/entries/freewill/ (accessed January 12, 2018).

Timpe, Kevin. (2008). *Free Will: Sourcehood and Its Alternatives.* London: Continuum.

van Inwagen, Peter. (1983). *An Essay on Free Will.* Oxford: Oxford University Press.

Watson, Gary, ed. (2003). *Free Will.* 2d ed. Oxford: Oxford University Press.

Widerker, David, and Michael McKenna, eds. (2003). *Moral Responsibility and Alternative Possibilities: Essays on the Importance of Alternative Possibilities.* Burlington, VT: Ashgate.

Wolf, Susan. (1990). *Freedom within Reason.* Oxford: Oxford University Press.

Ethics

Brink, David. (1989). *Moral Realism and the Foundations of Ethics.* Cambridge: Cambridge University Press.

Dancy, Jonathan. (1993). *Moral Reasons.* Oxford: Blackwell.

Harman, Gilbert. (1977). *The Nature of Morality: An Introduction to Ethics.* Oxford: Oxford University Press.

Joyce, Richard. (2001). *The Myth of Morality.* Cambridge: Cambridge University Press.

Korsgaard, Christine. (1996). *The Sources of Normativity.* New York: Cambridge University Press.

Loftin, R. Keith, ed. (2012). *God and Morality: Four Views.* Downers Grove, IL: InterVarsity Press.

Mackie, J. L. (1977). *Ethics: Inventing Right and Wrong.* New York: Penguin.

Ruse, Michael, and Robert J. Richards. (2017). *The Cambridge Handbook of Evolutionary Ethics.* Cambridge: Cambridge University Press.

Shafer-Landau, Russ. (2003). *Moral Realism: A Defence.* Oxford: Oxford University Press.

Smith, Michael. (1994). *The Moral Problem*. Oxford: Oxford University Press.

Wielenberg, Erik J. (2014). *Robust Ethics: The Metaphysics and Epistemology of Godless Normative Realism*. Oxford: Oxford University Press.

Wright, Robert. (1994). *The Moral Animal: Evolutionary Psychology and Everyday Life*. New York: Vintage Books.

BIBLIOGRAPHY

Adams, Marilyn McCord. (1999). *Horrendous Evils and the Goodness of God*. Ithaca: Cornell University Press.

Adams, Marilyn McCord. (2008). "Plantinga on 'Felix Culpa': Analysis and Critique." *Faith and Philosophy* 25: 123–39.

Adams, Robert. (1999). *Finite and Infinite Goods*. Oxford: Oxford University Press.

Adams, Marilyn, and Robert Adams, eds. (1991). *The Problem of Evil*. Oxford: Oxford University Press.

Anscombe, G. E. M. ([1957] 1981). "Mr. Truman's Degree." In *The Collected Philosophical Papers of G. E. M Anscombe*. Vol 3. *Ethics, Religion and Politics*, 62–71. Oxford: Blackwell Publishing.

Anselm. (1903). *Proslogium, Monologium, An Appendix on Behalf of the Fool by Gaunilo; and Cur Deus Homo*, trans. Sidney Norton Deane. Chicago: Open Court.

Aquinas, Thomas. (1947). *Summa Theologiae*, trans. Fathers of the English Dominican Province. New York: Benziger Brothers.

Aristotle. ([350 BCE] 1999). *Nicomachean Ethics*, trans. Martin Ostwald. Upper Saddle River, NJ: Prentice Hall.

Augustine. ([c.420] 1961.) *The Enchiridion on Faith, Hope, and Love*, trans. J. F. Shaw. Chicago: Regnery Publishing.

Augustine. ([400] 1993). *Confessions*. Rev. ed. Trans. F. J. Sheed. Indianapolis: Hackett.

Baldwin, Thomas. (1990). *G. E. Moore*. London: Routledge.

Barbour, Ian. (1990). *Religion in an Age of Science*. San Francisco: Harper & Row.

Bayne, Tim, and David Chalmers. (2003). "What is the Unity of Consciousness?" In *The Unity of Consciousness: Binding, Integration, Dissociation*, ed. Axel Cleeremans, 23–58. Oxford: Oxford University Press.

Bedke, Matthew. (2012). "Against Normative Naturalism." *Australasian Journal of Philosophy* 90: 111–29.

Bignon, Guillaume. (2018). *Excusing Sinners and Blaming God: A Calvinist Assessment of Determinism, Moral Responsibility, and Divine Involvement in Evil*. Eugene, OR: Pickwick Publications.

Blackburn, Simon. (1998). *Ruling Passions: A Theory of Practical Reasoning*. Oxford: Oxford University Press.

Brink, David. (1989). *Moral Realism and the Foundations of Ethics*. Cambridge: Cambridge University Press.

Burgess, Anthony. (1988). *A Clockwork Orange*. Rev. ed. New York: Ballantine Books.

Calder, Todd. (2002). "Toward a Theory of Evil Acts: A Critique of Laurence Thomas's Theory of Evil Acts." In *Earth's Abominations: Philosophical Studies of Evil*, ed. Daniel Haybron, 51–61. New York: Rodopi.

Calder, Todd. (2013). "Is Evil Just Very Wrong?" *Philosophical Studies* 163: 177–96.

Calvin, John. ([1559] 1960). *Institutes of the Christian Religion*, vol. 2, ed. John T. McNeill, trans. Ford Lewis Battles. Philadelphia: The Westminster Press.

Chalmers, David. (1996). *The Conscious Mind: In Search of a Fundamental Theory*. Oxford: Oxford University Press.

Churchland, Paul. (2013). *Matter and Consciousness: A Contemporary Introduction to the Philosophy of Mind*. 3rd ed. Cambridge, MA: MIT Press.

Clarke, Samuel. ([1705] 1998). *A Demonstration of the Being and Attributes of God*, ed. Ezio Vailati, Cambridge: Cambridge University Press.

Clarke, Samuel. (1708). *A Discourse Concerning the Unchangeable Obligations of Natural Religion and the Truth and Certainty of the Christian Revelation*. London: Printed for James Knapton at the Crown in St. Paul's Church-Yard.

Clarke, Samuel. (1717). *Remarks Upon a Book Entitled "A Philosophical Enquiry Concerning Human Liberty."* London: Printed for James Knapton at the Crown in St. Paul's Church-Yard.

Clarke, Samuel, and Anthony Collins. (2011). *The Correspondence of Samuel Clarke and Anthony Collins, 1707–1708*, ed. Wm. L. Uzgalis. Peterborough, ON: Broadview.

Cole, Phillip. (2006). *The Myth of Evil*. Edinburgh: Edinburgh University Press.

Craig, William Lane. (1994). *Reasonable Faith*. Rev. ed. Wheaton, IL: Crossway Books.

Crisp, Roger. (2006). *Reasons and the Good*. Oxford: Oxford University Press.

Darwin, Charles. (1859). *On the Origin of Species by Means of Natural Selection, or the Preservation of Favoured Races in the Struggle for Life*. London: John Murray.

Darwin, Charles. ([1860] 1993). *The Correspondence of Charles Darwin*. Vol 8. *1860*, eds. Frederick Burkhardt, Janet Browne, Duncan M. Porter, and Marsha Richmond. Cambridge: Cambridge University Press.

Darwin, Charles. (1861). *Origin of Species*. 3rd ed. London: John Murray.

Darwin, Charles. (1871). *The Descent of Man, and Selection in Relation to Sex*. Vol 1. London: John Murray.

Davis, Richard Brian, and W. Paul Franks. (2018). "Plantinga's Defence and His Theodicy are Incompatible." In *Does God Matter? Essays on the Axiological Consequences of Theism*, ed. Klaas J. Kraay, 203–23. New York: Routledge.

Dawkins, Richard. (1983). "Universal Darwinism." In *Evolution from Molecules to Men*, ed. D. S. Bendall, 403–25. Cambridge: Cambridge University Press.

Dawkins, Richard. (1995). *A River Out of Eden*. New York, NY: Basic Books.

Dawkins, Richard, and J. R. Krebs. (1979). "Arms Races Between and Within Species." *Proceedings of the Royal Society of London, B* 205: 489–511.

Dembski, William A., and Michael Ruse, eds. (2004). *Debating Design: Darwin to DNA*. Cambridge: Cambridge University Press.

Dennett, Daniel. (1984). *Elbow Room: The Varieties of Free Will Worth Wanting*. Cambridge, MA: MIT Press.

De Waal, Franz. (2005). *Our Inner Ape*. New York: Penguin.

Diller, Kevin. (2008). "Are Sin and Evil Necessary For a Really Good World? Questions for Alvin Plantinga's Felix Culpa Theodicy." *Faith and Philosophy* 25: 87–101.

Edwards, Jonathan. ([1741] 2008). "Sinners in the Hands of an Angry God." In *Works of Jonathan Edwards Online*. Vol. 22 *Sermons and Discourses, 1739–1742*, ed. Harry S. Stout. Jonathan Edwards Center, Yale University. Available online: edwards.yale.edu (accessed January 12, 2018).

Edwards, Jonathan. ([1754] 1957). *Works of Jonathan Edwards*. Vol. 1 *Freedom of Will*, ed. Paul Ramsey. New Haven: Yale University Press. Available online: edwards.yale.edu (accessed January 12, 2018).

Edwards, Jonathan. ([1754] 2017). *Freedom of the Will*, in the version by Jonathan Bennett presented at www.earlymoderntexts.com (accessed January 12, 2018).

Embury-Dennis, Tom. (2017). *The Independent*. February 9. Available online: http://www.independent.co.uk/news/world/europe/russian-newspaper-proud-bruises-vladimir-putin-domestic-abuse-violence-signs-controversial-law-a7570351.html (accessed January 12, 2018).

Enoch, David. (2007). "An Outline of an Argument for Robust Metanormative Realism." In *Oxford Studies in Metaethics*, Vol. 2, ed. Russ Shafer-Landau, 21–50. Oxford: Oxford University Press.

Enoch, David. (2011). *Taking Morality Seriously*. Oxford: Oxford University Press.

Epicurus. (1996). *A Guide to Happiness*. London: Phoenix Books; Abr. ed. *The Epicurean Philosophers*, ed. John Gaskin. London: Everyman Paperbacks, 1995.

Feldman, Fred. (2005). "The Open Question Argument: What It Isn't; And What It Is." *Philosophical Issues* 15: 22–43.

Fischer, John Martin, Robert Kane, Derk Pereboom, and Manuel Vargas. (2007). *Four Views on Free Will*. Malden, MA: Blackwell Publishing.

FitzPatrick, William (2008). "Robust Ethical Realism, Non-Naturalism, and Normativity." In *Oxford Studies in Metaethics*, Vol. 3, ed. Russ Shafer-Landau, 159–205. Oxford: Oxford University Press, 2008.

Fodor, Jerry, and Massimo Piattelli-Palmarini. (2010). *What Darwin Got Wrong*. New York: Farrar, Straus, and Giroux.

Frege, Gottlob. ([1884] 1980). *The Foundations of Arithmetic: A Logico-Mathematical Enquiry into the Concept of Number*, trans. J. L. Austin, 2nd rev. ed. Evanston, IL: Northwestern University Press.

Gould, Paul M., and Richard Brian Davis. (2014). "Modified Theistic Activism." In *Beyond the Control of God: Six Views on the Problem of God and Abstract Objects*, ed. Paul M. Gould, 51–64. New York: Bloomsbury Academic.

Greene, Brian. (2011). *The Hidden Reality: Parallel Universes and the Deep Laws of the Cosmos*. New York: Vintage Books.

Haldane, J. B. S. (1927). *Possible World and Other Essays*. London: Chatto & Windus.

Haldane, J. B. S. (1929). "The Origin of Life." In *The Rationalist Annual*, ed. Charles A. Watts, 3–10. Reprinted in J. B. S. Haldane, *Science and Life*. London: Pemberton Publishing, 1968.

Hare, Robert D. (1993). *Without Conscience: The Disturbing World of the Psychopaths among Us*. New York: Guilford Press.

Harman, Gilbert. (1977). *The Nature of Morality: An Introduction to Ethics*. Oxford: Oxford University Press.

Hasker, William. (1999). *The Emergent Self*. Ithaca: Cornell University Press.

Helm, Paul. (1988). *Eternal God: A Study of God without Time*. Oxford: Oxford University Press.

Helm, Paul. (1994). *Belief Policies*. Cambridge: Cambridge University Press.

Helm, Paul. (2000). *Faith with Reason*. Cambridge: Cambridge University Press.

Helm, Paul. (2001). "The Augustinian-Calvinist View." In *Divine Foreknowledge: Four Views*, eds. James K. Beilby and Paul R. Eddy, 161–89. Downers Grove, IL: InterVarsity Press.

Helm, Paul. (2010). "God, Compatibilism, and the Authorship of Sin." *Religious Studies* 46: 115–24.

Helm, Paul. (2015). "Human Beings, Compatibilist Freedom, and Salvation." In *The Ashgate Research Companion to Theological Anthropology*, eds. Joshua Farris and Charles Taliaferro, 245–60. Farnham, UK: Ashgate.

Hick, John. (1966). *Evil and the God of Love*. London: Macmillan.

Hitler, Adolf. ([1939] 2011) *Mein Kampf*, trans. James Murphy. Henley-in-Arden, United Kingdom: Coda Books Ltd.

Horgan, Terry, and Mark Timmons. (2007). "Morphological Rationalism and the Psychology of Moral Judgment." *Ethical Theory and Moral Practice* 10: 279–95.

Howard-Snyder, Daniel. (1996). "Introduction." In *The Evidential Argument from Evil*, ed. Daniel Howard-Snyder, xi–xx. Bloomington: Indiana University Press.

Hrdy, Sarah. (2009). *Mothers and Others: The Evolutionary Origins of Mutual Understanding*. Cambridge, MA: Harvard University Press.

Huemer, Michael. (2005). *Ethical Intuitionism*. New York: Palgrave Macmillan.

Huemer, Michael, and Ben Kovitz. (2003). "Causation as Simultaneous and Continuous." *The Philosophical Quarterly* 53: 556–65.

Hume, David. ([1739–40] 1978). *A Treatise of Human Nature*, ed. L. A. Selby-Bigge. 2nd ed. Rev. P. H. Nidditch. Oxford: Clarendon Press.

John Paul II. (1997). "The Pope's Message on Evolution." *Quarterly Review of Biology* 72: 381–83.

Kahneman, Daniel. (2011). *Thinking, Fast and Slow*. New York: Farrar, Straus and Giroux.

Kant, Immanuel. ([1785] 1993. *Grounding for the Metaphysics of Morals*. 3rd ed. Trans. James W. Ellington. Indianapolis: Hackett.

Kekes, John. (2005). *The Roots of Evil*. Ithaca: Cornell University Press.

Kennett, Jeanette, and Cordelia Fine. (2008). "Internalism and the Evidence from Psychopaths and 'Acquired Psychopaths.'" In *Moral Psychology* Vol 3. *The Neuroscience of Morality: Emotion, Brain Disorders, and Development*, ed. Walter Sinnott-Armstrong, 173–90. Cambridge, MA: MIT Press.

Kiehl, Kent A. (2014). *The Psychopath Whisperer: The Science of Those without Conscience*. New York: Broadway Books.

Koehn, Daryl. (2005). *The Nature of Evil*. New York: Palgrave Macmillan.

Kvanvig, Jonathan. (2008). "Creation and Conservation." In *The Stanford Encyclopedia of Philosophy* (Fall 2008 Edition), ed. Edward N. Zalta. Available online: http://plato.stanford.edu/archives/fall2008/entries/creation-conservation/ (accessed January 12, 2018).

Langtry, Bruce. (2008). *God, the Best, and Evil*. Oxford: Oxford University Press.

Larkin, Philip. 1974. *High Windows*. London: Faber & Faber.

Lewis, C. S. ([1940] 2001). *The Problem of Pain*. New York: HarperCollins.

Lewis, C. S. (1960). "The Cardinal Difficulty of Naturalism." In *Miracles*, 16–28. London: Fontana Books.

Lindbeck, George. (1984). *The Nature of Doctrine: Religion and Theology in a Postliberal Age*. Louisville: Westminster John Knox Press.

Locke, John. ([1689] 1975). *An Essay Concerning Human Understanding*. Oxford: Oxford University Press.

Mackie, J. L. (1977). *Ethics: Inventing Right and Wrong*. New York: Penguin.

Madueme, Hans. (2014). "The Most Vulnerable Part of the Whole Christian Account." In *Adam, the Fall, and Original Sin*, eds. Hans Madueme and Michael Reeves, 225–50. Grand Rapids, MI: Baker Academic.

McTaggart, J. M. E. (1906). *Some Dogmas of Religion*. London: Edward Arnold.

Meister, Chad. (2012). *Evil: A Guide for the Perplexed*. New York: Continuum.

Mikhail, John. (2011). *Elements of Moral Cognition*. Cambridge: Cambridge University Press.

Moore, George Edward. (1903). *Principia Ethica*. Cambridge: Cambridge University Press.

Moreland, J. P. (2013). "Exemplification and Constituent Realism: A Clarification and Modest Defense." *Axiomathes* 23: 247–59.

Moreland, James Porter, and William Lane Craig. (2003). *Philosophical Foundations for a Christian Worldview*. Downers Grove, IL: IVP Academic.

Morris, Simon Conway. (2003). *Life's Solution: Inevitable Humans in a Lonely Universe*. Cambridge: Cambridge University Press.

Murray, Michael, and Sean Greenberg. (2016). "Leibniz on the Problem of Evil." In *The Stanford Encyclopedia of Philosophy* (Winter 2016 Edition), ed. Edward N. Zalta. Available online: https://plato.stanford. edu/archives/win2016/entries/leibniz-evil/ (accessed January 12, 2018).

Nagel, Thomas. (1986). *The View from Nowhere*. Oxford: Oxford University Press.

Nagel, Thomas. (2012). *Mind and Cosmos: Why the Materialist Neo-Darwinian Conception of Nature is Almost Certainly False*. Oxford: Oxford University Press.

Nelson, Mark T. (1991). "Naturalistic Ethics and the Argument from Evil." *Faith and Philosophy* 8: 368–79.

Niebuhr, Reinhold. (1941). *The Nature and Destiny of Man*. Vol. 1, *Human Nature*. New York: Charles Scribner's Sons.

Niebuhr, Reinhold. (1943). *The Nature and Destiny of Man*. Vol. 2, *Human Destiny*. New York: Charles Scribner's Sons.

Nietzsche, Friedrich. ([1895] 1990). "The Anti-Christ." In *Twilight of Idols and Anti-Christ*, trans. R. J. Hollingdale. London: Penguin Books.

Nozick, Robert. (1981). *Philosophical Explanations*. Cambridge, MA: Harvard University Press.

Numbers, Ronald L. (2006). *The Creationists: From Scientific Creationism to Intelligent Design*. Exp. ed. Cambridge, MA: Harvard University Press.

O'Connor, Timothy. (1995). "Agent Causation." In *Agents, Causes, and Events: Essays on Indeterminism and Free Will*, ed. Timothy O'Connor, 173–200. Oxford: Oxford University Press.

O'Connor, Timothy. (2000). *Persons and Causes: The Metaphysics of Free Will*. Oxford: Oxford University Press.

O'Connor, Timothy, and Hong Yu Wong. (2005). "The Metaphysics of Emergence." *Nous* 39: 658–78.

Parfit, Derek. (2011a). *On What Matters, Volume I*. Oxford: Oxford University Press.

Parfit, Derek. (2011b). *On What Matters, Volume II*. Oxford: Oxford University Press.

Pereboom, Derk. (2007). "Hard Incompatibilism." In *Four Views on Free Will*, eds. John Martin Fischer, Robert Kane, Derk Pereboom, and Manuel Vargas, 85–125. Malden, MA: Blackwell Publishing.

Peterson, Michael L. (2012). "Christian Theism and the Evidential Argument from Evil." In *Philosophy and the Christian Worldview*, eds. David Werther and Mark Linville, 175–95. New York: Continuum.

Plantinga, Alvin. (1967). *God and Other Minds*. Ithaca: Cornell University Press.

Plantinga, Alvin. (1974a). *God, Freedom, and Evil*. Grand Rapids, MI: Wm. B. Eerdmans Publishing.

Plantinga, Alvin. (1974b). *The Nature of Necessity*. Oxford: Oxford University Press.

Plantinga, Alvin. (1993). *Warrant and Proper Function*. Oxford: Oxford University Press.

Plantinga, Alvin (1991). "When Faith and Reason Clash: Evolution and the Bible." *Christian Scholar's Review* 21: 8–32. Reprinted in *The Philosophy of Biology*, eds. D. Hull and M. Ruse, 674–97. Oxford: Oxford University Press, 1998.

Plantinga, Alvin. (2004). "Supralapsarianism, or 'O Felix Culpa.'" In *Christian Faith and the Problem of Evil*, ed. Peter van Inwagen, 1–25. Grand Rapids, MI: Wm. B. Eerdmans Publishing.

Plantinga, Alvin. (2011). *Where the Conflict Really Lies: Science, Religion, and Naturalism*. Oxford: Oxford University Press.

Quine, Willard van Orman, and J. S. Ullian. (1978). *The Web of Belief*. New York: Random House.

Rachels, James. (1991). *Created from Animals: The Moral Implications of Darwinism*. Oxford: Oxford University Press.

Reppert, Victor. (2009). "The Argument from Reason." In *The Blackwell Companion to Natural Theology*, eds. William Lane Craig and J. P. Moreland, 344–90. Malden, MA: Blackwell Publishing.

Richards, Robert. (1986). "A Defense of Evolutionary Ethics." *Biology and Philosophy* 1: 265–93.

Roberts, Jon H. (1988). *Darwinism and the Divine in America: Protestant Intellectuals and Organic Evolution, 1859–1900*. Madison, WI: University of Wisconsin Press.

Ruben, David-Hillel. (1990). *Explaining Explanation*. London: Routledge.

Ruse, Michael. (1979). *Sociobiology: Sense or Nonsense?* Dordrecht, Holland: Reidel.

Ruse, Michael. (1986). *Taking Darwin Seriously: A Naturalistic Approach to Philosophy*. Oxford: Blackwell Publishing.

Ruse, Michael. (1995). "Evolutionary Ethics: A Phoenix Arisen." In *Issues in Evolutionary Ethics*, ed. Paul Thompson, 225–47. Buffalo: SUNY Press.

Ruse, Michael. (1996). *Monad to Man: The Concept of Progress in Evolutionary Biology*. Cambridge, MA: Harvard University Press.

Ruse, Michael. (2001). *Can a Darwinian be a Christian? The Relationship between Science and Religion*. Cambridge: Cambridge University Press.

Ruse, Michael. (2005). *The Evolution-Creation Struggle*. Cambridge, MA: Harvard University Press.

Ruse, Michael. (2008). *Charles Darwin*. Oxford: Blackwell Publishing.

Ruse, Michael. (2012a). *The Philosophy of Human Evolution*. Cambridge: Cambridge University Press.

Ruse, Michael. (2012b). "Naturalist Moral Nonrealism." In *God and Morality: Four Views*, ed. R. Keith Loftin, 53–96. Downers Grove, IL: InterVarsity Press.

Ruse, Michael. (2013). *The Gaia Hypothesis: Science on a Pagan Planet*. Chicago: University of Chicago Press.

Ruse, Michael. (2015). *Atheism: What Everyone Needs to Know*. Oxford: Oxford University Press.

Ruse, Michael. (2017a). *Darwinism as Religion: What Literature Tells Us about Evolution*. Oxford: Oxford University Press.

Ruse, Michael. (2017b). *On Purpose*. Princeton: Princeton University Press.

Ruse, Michael. (2018). *Darwinism and War: Science or Religion?* Oxford: Oxford University Press.

Ruse, Michael, and Edward O. Wilson. (1985). "The Evolution of Morality." *New Scientist* 1478: 108–28.

Ruse, Michael, and Robert J. Richards. (2017). *The Cambridge Handbook of Evolutionary Ethics*. Cambridge: Cambridge University Press.

Scarre, Geoffrey. (2009). "The Wrong that is Right? The Paradox of the 'Felix Culpa.'" In *The Positive Function of Evil*, ed. P. A. Tabensky, 14–27. New York: Palgrave Macmillan.

Segerstrale, Ullica. (1986). "Colleagues in Conflict: An 'in vivo' Analysis of the Sociobiology Controversy." *Biology and Philosophy* 1: 53–88.

Shafer-Landau, Russ. (2003). *Moral Realism: A Defence*. Oxford: Oxford University Press.

Singer, Peter. (1972). "Famine, Affluence, and Morality." *Philosophy and Public Affairs* 1: 229–43.

Smith, David Livingstone. (2011). *Less than Human: Why We Demean, Enslave, and Exterminate Others*. New York: St. Martin's Press.

Spencer, Herbert. (1879). *The Data of Ethics*. London: Williams and Norgate.

Stout, Martha. (2005). *The Sociopath Next Door*. New York: Broadway Books.

Stump, Eleonore. (2010). *Wandering in Darkness: Narrative and the Problem of Suffering*. Oxford: Oxford University Press.

Stump, Eleonore. (2012). "The Nature of the Atonement." In *Reason, Metaphysics, and Mind: New Essays on the Philosophy of Alvin Plantinga*, eds. Kelly James Clark and Michael Rea, 128–44. Oxford: Oxford University Press.

Swinburne, Richard. (1977). *The Coherence of Theism*. Oxford: Oxford University Press.

Swinburne, Richard. (1998). *Providence and the Problem of Evil*. Oxford: Oxford University Press.

Thomas, Laurence. (1993). *Vessels of Evil: American Slavery and the Holocaust*. Philadelphia: Temple University Press.

Trakakis, Nick. (2005). "Is Theism Capable of Accounting for Any Natural Evil at All?" *International Journal for Philosophy of Religion* 57: 35–66.

van Inwagen, Peter. (2006). *The Problem of Evil*. Oxford: Oxford University Press.

van Inwagen, Peter. (2013). "C.S. Lewis's Argument Against Naturalism." *Res Philosophica* 90: 113–24.

Waller, James. (2007). *Becoming Evil: How Ordinary People Commit Genocide and Mass Killing*. 2nd ed. Oxford: Oxford University Press.

Watts, Isaac. ([1724] 1996). *Logic: The Right Use of Reason in the Inquiry After Truth*. Morgan, PA: Soli Deo Gloria Publications.

Wielenberg, Erik J. (2005). *Value and Virtue in a Godless Universe.* Cambridge: Cambridge University Press.

Wielenberg, Erik J. (2008). *God and the Reach of Reason: C. S. Lewis, David Hume, and Bertrand Russell.* Cambridge: Cambridge University Press.

Wielenberg, Erik J. (2014). *Robust Ethics: The Metaphysics and Epistemology of Godless Normative Realism.* Oxford: Oxford University Press.

Wilson, Edward O. (1975). *Sociobiology: The New Synthesis.* Cambridge, MA: Harvard University Press.

Wilson, Timothy. (2002). *Strangers to Ourselves: Discovering the Adaptive Unconscious.* Cambridge, MA: Harvard University Press.

Wright, Robert. (1994). *The Moral Animal: Evolutionary Psychology and Everyday Life.* New York: Vintage Books.

INDEX